François Jean

From Ethiopia to Chechnya

Reflections on Humanitarian Action 1988-1999

MEDECINS SANS FRONTIERES
DOCTORS WITHOUT BORDERS

Edited by Kevin P.Q. Phelan
Translated by Richard Swanson

The Médecins Sans Frontières Charter

Médecins Sans Frontières/Doctors Without Borders (MSF) offers assistance to populations in distress, victims of natural or man-made disasters, and victims of armed conflict, without discrimination and irrespective of race, religion, creed, or political affiliation.

MSF observes strict neutrality and impartiality in the name of universal medical ethics and the right to humanitarian assistance, and demands full and unhindered freedom in the exercise of its functions.

MSF volunteers undertake to observe their professional code of ethics and to maintain complete independence from all political, economic, and religious powers.

Volunteers are aware of the risks and dangers of the missions they undertake and have no right to compensation for themselves or their beneficiaries other than that which MSF is able to afford them.

ISBN: 978-0-9747145-1-6

Contents

iv   Preface

v   Introduction

Section One
Famine

2   Famine and Ideology (1988)

13   Ethiopia: A Political Famine (1988)

24   North Korea: A Famine Regime (1999)

Section Two
Conflict

50   Security: How Do We Know When Not to Go Too Far? (1991)

53   Have You Heard About Somalia? (1992)

56   The Sudanese Conflict (1993)

59   What Role for MSF? (1993)

61   Necessary Independence (1997)

63   Mission Impossible...On the Back Roads of Chechnya (1996)

66   The Problems of Medical Relief in Chechen War Zones* (1996)

71   Chechnya: Moscow's Revenge, Statistics Included* (2000)

Section Three
International Aid

82   Life, Death, and Aid*(1993)

93   Europe, Refugees, and War (1994)

107   Humanitarian Action and Politics: A Marriage from Hell (1994)

114   Compromised Humanitarian Action? (1994)

125   From State-to-State to Transnational: The Role of Non-State Actors in Conflicts (The Case of International Humanitarian Organizations) (1998)

157   Humanitarian Action: Image, Perception, and Security (1998)

* English original

Preface

François Jean left a mark on Médecins Sans Frontières. He was probably the only one who didn't know this, as he hated drawing attention to himself. He also probably would have asked why in the world we decided to gather the texts and discussions he had given over the course of 17 years of work with MSF. He was not concerned with his legacy, which is why he never went to the trouble of collecting his works in one place. This was only made possible because of the great patience and tenacity of Cécile Lapérou, and then Marie Le Page. They deserve wholehearted thanks.

Their editing reveals his piercing insight into the key situations and themes that marked the evolution of contemporary humanitarian action. François explored, questioned, and shed light on the field of international aid, from the famine in Ethiopia to the one in North Korea, from the Lome accords to the right of intervention, from humanitarians in war zones to humanitarian wars. Far from moralizing, animated by a permanent restlessness about action and its uncertainties, he always remained a calm and lucid practitioner, anxious to understand and to act, without ever sacrificing one to the other. The texts that follow attest to the fruitfulness of his doubts and the relevance of his critical reflections.

François put an end to his own days on December 25, 1999—a dark day, a day of storms. The homage we pay him here in the form of a publication is not an act of piety but rather one of profound and sincere recognition. Thank you, François, for who you were, for what you brought to us, and for what you have left us.

Rony Brauman, 2004

(Translated from the French by Kevin P.Q. Phelan)

Introduction

Necessary Memory: François Jean and Humanitarian Action

For nearly two decades, François Jean practiced humanitarian action based on a deep, pragmatic desire to understand, constant self-questioning, and broad intellectual curiosity. It will be clear to anyone reading his collected works, *From Ethiopia to Chechnya: Reflections on Humanitarian Action, 1988-1999*, that his meditations resonate with dilemmas we face today.

In the essays that start the book, Jean examined the political roots of famines in Ukraine and China from the first half of the 20th century and saw similar forces at work in Ethiopia and North Korea in the 1980s and 1990s. Both regimes prolonged the crises by perversely manipulating the food assistance pouring into the famine-wracked countries. The ideology underpinning these actions allowed for the sacrifice of tens of thousands of people in exchange for the promise of a radiant, future utopia. In such contexts, Jean wrote, it was imperative for humanitarian aid organizations to closely monitor the delivery of assistance lest they "fund a lunatic project of social transformation."

Fast-forward to 2005 and the central African country Niger. As a nutritional crisis deepened there, development organizations and donor countries initially argued against providing emergency food aid because it might negatively affect long-term projects. Thus, the not-yet-born were privileged over those who were actually dying.

Such calculations would have been obscene to Jean, for whom humanitarian action is, at its core, an act of human cooperation and solidarity—not an ideology. Nor is it a mere technocratic exercise of efficiently stuffing "digestive apparatuses" with food and medicines—such a stance "can breed attitudes of arrogance and contempt." Rather, for Jean, the humanitarian's goal should be to help "people in times of acute crisis reestablish their capacities for choice."

François Jean joined Médecins Sans Frontières (MSF) in 1982 to establish and run medical surgical programs in Lebanon, and he made an immediate impression on people for his ability to navigate a country convulsed by war. Relying on a nuanced analysis of the chaotic situation, an innate talent for negotiating, and sheer common sense, he managed to pass through all of the checkpoints set up by a dizzying array of warring parties—Palestinian, Christian, pro- and anti-Syrian, as well as factions within these factions—to bring a measure of medical relief to people trapped by the fighting.

He would continue for the next 17 years in the field and at headquarters to make important contributions to the evolution and direction of MSF operations, with people running emergency medical aid programs seeking his advice and insights—from Afghanistan, Central Asia, and Kurdistan, to the former Yugoslavia, Sudan, Somalia, and Ethiopia. He played an especially key role in helping resolve hostage situations in Chechnya and Tajikistan in the early and mid-1990s.

Jean wrote prolifically during his time with MSF for internal publications as well as for a variety of magazines and journals about the difficulties and challenges faced by humanitarian aid workers. He helped create and edit the series *Populations in Danger*, a collection of essays that wrestled with defining the scope and limits of humanitarian action. The series was, according to Dr. Rony Brauman, president of MSF's French section from 1982 to 1996, "the first attempt by MSF to establish a global framework of our work in war-torn nations." Jean also co-founded MSF's *Fondation*, a center for reflection on humanitarian action based in Paris, after being the lead researcher for MSF's short-lived *Liberté Sans Frontières* project.

All of these efforts had a clear operational focus: how to overcome the practical constraints to delivering meaningful assistance to people trying to survive crises, particularly in times of conflict. When war broke out in Chechnya in 1996, Jean wrote how the team in Grozny was "trapped by the fighting without much in the way of resources." Instead of staying on the sidelines, they left the city on foot, trudged medical supplies through fields around Russian checkpoints, and in the end helped hundreds of war wounded to receive treatment even as the city was laid to waste by indiscriminate bombings and intense fighting.

This impulse to act was never reckless, though, and Jean wrote at length about the need to weigh the risks involved in delivering aid. He cautions us to never forget that we are outsiders—carrying a good deal of money, no less—in volatile and fluid situations dominated by nervous armed men, where our own self-preservation is the obvious prerequisite for continued action. Real security, Jean felt, was elusive and not simply evacuation procedures and context analysis, but "the result of day-to-day conduct, of understanding a society, and of being able to size up situations."

As the shadow of the Cold War receded, the nature of conflicts changed and the aid system itself underwent a serious transformation. Jean struggled to understand this new landscape and MSF's role within it. Manipulation of aid grew more subtle while conflicts fragmented and revealed the localized antagonisms that had been obscured by East-West proxy battles. There was a massive proliferation of aid groups running programs closer and closer to the center of conflicts. Refugees lost the political significance they had in the West during the Cold War, and now people fleeing conflicts were actively kept in war zones and called "economic migrants." The diminishing importance of state-to-state interactions in these areas was coupled with the increasing influence of non-state actors—not only nongovernmental organizations (NGOs), but also gun-runners in search of new markets and multinational corporations bent on securing diamonds, oil, and other natural resources.

During these years, the United Nations became much more assertive in deploying military force, often becoming a party to conflicts while consigning relief efforts to a supporting role to political and military objectives. Western governments found that the humanitarian label could pay political dividends while masking political-military actions, or semblance of action. As the lines between military engagement and humanitarian action blurred, Jean saw quickly how aid organizations sometimes helped accelerate the process. By relying disproportionately on government funding to run programs, many groups were simply becoming subcontractors beholden to the shifting political winds of their benefactors. And the calls from groups, including MSF, for the "international community" to engage in crises often bore strange fruit. In Somalia, "it only resulted in reducing the space for humanitarian action, because the Somalis have consistently lumped NGOs together with the UN army that landed under the humanitarian banner."

How best to provide emergency medical assistance in these environments? For Jean, the twin principles of independence and impartiality would be our best guides. Not as rigid words to be worn like badges—let alone bulletproof vests—but as values aid workers must wrestle with and put into practice in their daily activities and decisions. Otherwise, our credibility, especially with the people we were trying to assist, would be lost. "The impression we have been able to gather on the ground," he wrote after having completed scores of field assignments, "would indicate that, at best, humanitarian organizations are viewed as importers of all-terrain vehicles, at worst as a new affluent class. Likewise, everything leads one to believe they are perceived either as agents of their governments or the West—in any event as actors with political agendas and influence."

We are confronted with similar challenges today … Somalia, Iraq, Afghanistan—even some of the countries have not changed. And though Jean's writings reveal a sharp intelligence, the essays here have an intimate and personal quality, as if he were in conversation with other aid workers—not making academic assessments of institutions and events. His writing bristles with calls for those engaged in humanitarian action to be vigilant in "the capacity for self-questioning." If not, "self-righteous rhetoric, good intentions, and moralistic posing can become a kind of ambient background noise, dulling our vigilance and deadening our awareness of our responsibilities."

Aid worker, writer, and, to those who knew him in life, friend. While many of us never met François Jean, the works collected here offer insight into the man, his actions, and his thoughts. Perhaps more important, his astute and lively works continue to speak to the situations we encounter in the field, forming a legacy to be emulated and animating the belief that we can act most clearly in the present when we reflect on the past. After all, as he reminds us, "our ignorance exacts a heavy toll …."

Kevin P.Q. Phelan,
March 2008

Section One
Famine

Chapter One

Famine And Ideology

Originally published in *Commentaire*, No. 42, summer 1988, p. 444-449

The black earth was sown with bones
and sprinkled with blood
for a harvest of sorrow
in the land of Rus'

The Tale of Igor's Armament (12th century)

These prophetic lines open a recent work devoted to one of the most neglected aspects of contemporary history: famine.[1] Famine we see on our TV screens from time to time is all the more intolerable because it seems a vestige of a long-ago age. But this is far from the case. During the 20th century famine caused as many deaths as did conflicts between nations. How many of us, indeed, are aware that one famine in Ukraine and the Northern Caucasus alone killed as many peasants as all the combatants killed during World War I? How many, for that matter, realize that the victims of the "Great Leap Forward" were equal in number to either civilian or military losses in Europe during World War II? How many of us, finally, know that the toll of the 1984–85 famine in Ethiopia is probably as heavy—though only for the moment heaven knows—as that of the Iran-Iraq conflict? We end this ghoulish tally, worth reciting only to allay our astonishing ignorance of these events. The Ethiopian disaster wasn't big enough to hold our attention for very long, certainly. Compared to war, deeply rooted in the Western imagination as the symbol of absolute evil, famine touches our awareness only sporadically. Tragic images of starving children break our hearts, soon to vanish in the onrush of the news cycle.

---

[1] Robert Conquest, *The Harvest of Sorrow* (Oxford University Press, 1986).

In this awkward encounter with uttermost distress, any sort of analysis seems unnecessary. Indeed, with thousands of studies devoted to wars and conflict, it is hard to cite even a small number of books on famines, most familiar only to specialists. Many of these tragedies slipped by unnoticed, to be sure, because the facts were long concealed. For example, it was necessary to wait until the post-World War II period and its flood of refugees, along with the half truths later revealed during de-Stalinization, for the Ukrainian slaughter to appear in its fullest dimensions. Similarly, the most prescient fears of "China-watchers" concerning the toll of the 1959–61 famine would not be confirmed until 20 years later, with the availability of previously unpublished demographic data. Yet even as witness accounts pile up and catastrophes become clearly legible in the official statistics themselves, indifference prevails over fresh evidence. The burden of forgetting weighs especially heavy, because it buries historical lessons essential to our understanding of this century's worst famines.

Politically-Inspired Famines

Just as war-making has spread far beyond the battlefield over the last half century, famine also has increased significantly in scale and destructive capacity. The number of persons that starved in the Russian famines of 1891, 1906, and 1919, which never exceeded 3 million across all Russian territories, scarcely approaches the number threatened by the 1921 famine in the Soviet Union (13 million), or that of 1933 (almost 30 million in Ukraine alone). The mortality rate recorded at the time of the Ukrainian famine was unprecedented, as well: one-fifth of the population died in this breadbasket of Central Europe. Similarly, the number of victims of China's Great Leap Forward exceeded—and by a large margin—those of the Chinese famines of the 19th and the first half of the 20th centuries. A new type of famine emerged during the ordeal of China's "dark years" between 1959–61, one that not only struck in every part of the country, but did so for three years running, an unprecedented phenomenon. Finally, the Ethiopian famine of 1984–85 probably caused three times the number of deaths than the earlier famine in 1972–1973. In any event it was nothing similar to the Sahelian famines, with victims numbering in the thousands, not hundreds of thousands.

Many suspect that these famines were less a consequence of climate than of politics; certain Chinese and Ethiopian leaders have indeed acknowledged as much. Nor were these famines linked to a state of war—except in Ethiopia, which was a war between the State and the peasantry. Only one side was armed, though, and all the victims were peasants. Breaking with a thousand-year tradition of retail massacre, the 20th century ushered in the era of mass extermination. Ordinary carnage has given way to magnificent projects of "social prophylaxis" in which orchestrated elimination of the "old" society has, on occasion, been taken to its most extreme consequences. For famine has not only changed in scale, it has changed in nature. What was once a timeless scourge, a natural calamity, has become a phenomenon of the modern age and an act of government; no longer part of the toll of war, it has become an offering on the altar of ideology.

The Ethiopian famine provides a remarkable illustration of this development. The result of drought, war, and the regime's policies, it is a situation of uncommon complexity combining the traditional attributes of previous famines with newer features that reached their consummate form in the USSR and, later, in China. The same ordeal is replaying itself 50 years later under the incredulous gaze of TV-watchers equipped, so to speak, with high-powered binoculars for the occasion. Not because the events are similar in their cause, scale, or ramifications, but because they proceed from the same view of reality, the same vision of the future, the same exaggerated urge to transform society. Apart from obvious distinctions, the same logic is at work—one that would plunge the three countries into unprecedented disasters.

Politically-Inspired Famines: The Numbers

Estimates of the toll of the 1984–85 Ethiopian famine run from 600,000 to 1 million dead, a "bracket" roughly equal to losses in the Iran-Iraq conflict between 1980 and 1986. For the two world wars we based our conclusions on the Soviet specialist B. Ourlanis. This data has been challenged at times for overestimating Soviet losses, in the opinion of most analysts, but offers the advantage of providing an overall summary. Ourlanis estimates the number of soldiers killed in combat in 1914–18 at 6 million, and the excess mortality associated with World War II in Europe at 26 million (not counting the millions of victims of Nazi concentration and extermination camps). For the Great Leap Forward, the demographer G. Calot estimates the number of victims of the Great Famine (1959–61) at 28 million, based on data provided by China after the 1982 census.

For the Ukrainian famine (1932–33), the absence of official data makes analysis difficult. Based on a comparison of the censuses of 1926 and 1939, and assuming "normal" demographic growth during that period, the most conservative observers (R. Conquest, J. Mace, etc.) put the number of victims of the rural terror at 14.5 million in the Soviet Union during the 1930s, with 6.5 million of these associated with de-*kulakization*, 1 million linked to collectivization in Kazakhstan, and 7 million due to the 1932–33 famine (6 million of that number in Ukraine and the North Caucasus). This assessment clearly underestimates the true toll: the 1939 census was actually preceded by a never-published 1937 census whose authors were promptly liquidated for having "minimized the USSR's population figure." One imagines that their 1939 successors did not wish to take any further risks and set to work filling in the gaps … As Stalin said, "The death of one man is a tragedy; the disappearance of thousands is a statistic." With the statistics duly "corrected," the famine, now reduced to the status of "hypothesis," disappeared from memory.

The Party and the Peasant

Utopians view the peasant either as angel or animal: a repository of the nation's soul, an identity figure embodying the mythical values of a golden age not yet corrupted by monetary exchange and colonial domination—or the opposite: "totally devoid of social consciousness" according to Gorki, who excoriated the "animal individualism of the peasant." The Khmer Rouge carried the former view, much-prized by champions of authenticity, to the point of madness. City dwellers and peasants alike were engulfed in a lunatic project of social regeneration. The latter view lay behind the massive Soviet slaughters: it merits closer attention because it is at the core of the same hysteria for development that held the seeds of Ethiopia's ordeal.

Avant-garde revolutionaries, to be sure, have no monopoly on contempt for "backward," individualistic peasants, supposedly incapable of acting rationally. It is intrinsic to the rhetoric of development wielded by clients of state patronage to legitimize its power and justify its policies. In many countries the peasantry is seen as a shapeless mass, useless except as a resource to be tapped for the nation's construction and industrial development. However, in some cases this contempt, widely shared among third world industrializing elites, is paired with an intent to transform persons and societies. "The numbing mindlessness of peasant life"…Marx's perfunctory condemnation, in aid of his appeal for a capitalism that would hasten social and technological differentiation, quickly grew into a menacing bogeyman for preachers, great and small, of the true socialism. The image of the *kulak* now replaced that of the *mujik*, and the primitive peasant was transformed into a class enemy, to be dealt with by the radical measures Stalin described in April 1930: "Our policy is to liquidate the kulak as a social class. We have tolerated these bloodsuckers, these scorpions and vampires. Now we have the opportunity to replace them with our economy of *kolkhozes* and *sovkhozes*." Exit the reactionary, inefficient peasantry; enter mechanized, "scientific" agriculture. We know the economic consequences of this tremendous upheaval, but the human disaster it represented is too often forgotten. Peasants ended up propped atop tractors or stacked in open graves. Repression of the countryside took the form of mass deportations and unprecedented famines.

More than a half century after the massive transformation Stalin decreed, the cult of the tractor and the myth of the agricultural factory remain intact. As a vehicle of progress the tractor is to socialist agriculture what the magic wand is to fairy tales: sputtering and backfiring in all its modernity, bristling with red flags, and draped with propagandists, it proclaims to the village the new era pledged by its leaders, plowing the furrows of the radiant future to come across the horizons of propaganda posters lining the traffic intersections of Kiev or Addis Ababa. Together with this faith in technology is an unflagging infatuation with large-scale industrial agriculture. Colonel Mengistu's official statements are akin to those of Stalin in their vision of a future centered upon large agricultural complexes crisscrossed by tractor stations, work brigades, and housing cooperatives … Over the years, the debates between Bukharin and Stalin over the pace and logistics of collectivization have yielded way to a radical approach. Strumilin's maxim "Our task is not to study the economy but to change it"—which condemned Bukharin and other "bourgeois-kulak ideologues" to early purges—can now be cited in prefaces of Bulgarian manuals that feed military-progressive fantasies of ready-made formulas for sweeping development.

As it turned out, however, this pseudo-industrialization quickly developed into out-and-out bureaucratization, the would-be economies of scale into large-scale waste—as Khrushchev acknowledged in 1953 when he declared that scientific agriculture produced less grain per inhabitant than the mujiks of old, with their wooden plows. Colonel Mengistu likewise admits that state farm productivity is no greater than that of traditional peasants ... then goes on to urge speeding up collectivization. Clearly the leadership in Addis Ababa grasps neither the suicidal character of its policies, nor the failure of Soviet agriculture, nor even the fresh doubts surrounding China's people's communes—the last projected phase of Ethiopian cooperatives.

The lure of the Stalinist model owes less to its efficiency—highly dubious—than to the fact that it furnishes a program for development and an organizing framework that is greatly reassuring to leaders hungry for progress. It is equally appealing because of the opportunities it creates for social control in countries where the peasantry is for the most part still "un-captured."

In most cases, collectivization has primarily been an expedient for policing or extracting resources; apart from ideological motivations, it has been a handy instrument for tightening the state's grip on populations and their production. It is significant that whenever collectivization was stepped up in China and the USSR, the cause was inadequate food supply. Wherever it occurs, collectivization, along with famine, seems to be the crowning phase of a project aimed at subjugating peasants, once and for all, to the power of the state and the party.

Ukraine: Extermination by Hunger
In the case of Ukraine, this desire to control, coupled with an utter inability to comprehend how a rural economy functions, degenerated into all-out war against the peasantry. The 1921 famine in the USSR was due less to climate than to the exactions of "War Communism." This massive

famine, which claimed more than five million victims, was the outcome of a deadly cycle of confiscations, revolt, and repression that would have been completely lost to memory were it not for the legendary figure Makhno. Requisitions of harvests—misleadingly termed surpluses—left peasants totally destitute in the face of climate crisis, plunging them into famine. The scale of the disaster and the precariousness of the situation prompted the Communist Party to pause in its campaign to repress of the countryside. The New Economic Policy (NEP) provided a structure more favorable to peasant production, until sub-par quota deliveries due to dissuasive pricing policies prompted a harsh regime response. In 1925, 30,000 party militants descended on the countryside to seize the grain quotas demanded by planning authorities. The sweeping confiscation was a success for the government: the requisite quantities were indeed collected and the party thereby concluded it was easier to seize grain by command than to obtain it via market forces. But peasants saw these extortionate measures, which recalled the methods of War Communism only too well, as proof that the NEP's liberalizing reforms were unreliable. Production incentives, already weakened by frequent policy changes, were permanently undermined. The consequent decline in production immediately led to new requisition campaigns, on the supposition that kulaks, now permanently elevated to the status of saboteurs, were withholding huge grain reserves.

While peasants were being deported or collectivized en masse, the countryside, bled white by the "Bread Procurement Commission," sank into deep poverty. Despite all efforts, grain collections were below quota year after year, hardening the party's determination and reinforcing the cycle of repression. In the summer of 1932, collectivized and bled dry, Ukraine was once again presented with unachievable goals. One last "battle for production" was launched under the aegis of the GPU [predecessor of the KGB], officially responsible for eliminating saboteurs, prohibiting any resupply of kolkhozes that had not fulfilled their quotas, and ensuring the success of the harvest—now designated the "sacred and inviolable" property of the state. From then on Ukraine's fate was sealed. The winter of 1933 was horrifying; hordes of emaciated peasants could be seen combing the countryside, unearthing animal carcasses outside well-stocked warehouses. Militia fired on sight at the starving caught digging in the frozen soil in search of grain or potatoes. Militants searched relentlessly among the dead and dying for "hidden wheat," busily in walls, knocking on floors, and harassing survivors, who were suspected—by virtue simply of having survived—of diverting government assets for their personal benefit. Survivors' accounts are replete with extraordinary scenes[2] such as these, the crowning moment of a calculated policy designed to liquidate peasants as a social class and Ukrainians as a nation. The Ukrainian tragedy is a remarkable illustration of a famine deliberately created and coldly planned down to its ultimate consequences. It was probably the first of the hidden genocides that eliminated millions of people, in silence, in the very heart of Europe.

Herriot's Perspicacity

Denial of the facts, backed up by a healthy dose of disinformation, was enough to securely reassure a public little inclined, naturally, to accept the unacceptable. Still, as occurred later during the Holocaust, proof of the worst was very soon confirmed. Despite a blackout imposed in Ukraine there was no shortage of witness accounts; these were systematically denied by the Soviet authorities. Offers of aid were rejected as imperialist propaganda. Trips were organized in order to refute the "lies of the bourgeois press," and former French Prime Minister Édouard Herriot was invited to tour the trompe l'oeil scenes of Potemkin villages, where GPU agents disguised as peasants bestirred themselves cheerfully. After viewing this skillfully orchestrated production, Herriot, only too willing to be convinced, felt entitled to declare, "You'll pardon me if I shrug my shoulders when they claim the Ukraine is being devastated by famine." A shrug of the shoulders for 6 million dead ... In fairness to Édouard Herriot, others—without the benefit of ignorance—assented obligingly to the operation.[3] "Enlightened" opinion of the day all but asked to be deceived.

---

[2] Miron Dolot, *Execution by Hunger: The Hidden Holocaust* (New York: W.W. Norton & Co., 1985).

[3] Marco Carynnyk, "The Famine the Times Couldn't Find," *Commentary* 76, November 1983. See also James W. Crowd, *Angels in Stalin's Paradise: Western Reporters in Soviet Russia, 1917 to 1937* (University Press of America, 1982).

Ethiopia: Headlong Rush

Nothing of the sort occurred in Ethiopia. The famine there was ultimately acknowledged, and international assistance actively solicited. Clearly the Ethiopian famine is more the outcome of the combined effects of drought and war than of a deliberate use of hunger to crush the peasantry. In Eritrea and Tigre the long-running conflict between Addis Ababa and guerilla movements left peasants at the mercy of drought and plunged them hopelessly into famine. In these regions especially sensitive to the vagaries of climate, the ravages of war and the army's exactions have disrupted agricultural production, weakened rural social structures, and paralyzed relief operations. Over the years famine has come to be used as a weapon, food aid as a trump card to weaken opposition movements and control populations. The situation is not new: throughout history famine has followed in the wake of tanks and at times has come before. Still, famine would never have reached this degree of severity if those regions untouched by the conflict had not already been weakened by the regime's social experiments. For 10 years all of Ethiopia has been mired in chronic food scarcity and increasing dependence on international aid. The situation derives neither from a hostile climate, unforgiving soil, nor the alleged primitivism of Ethiopia's peasantry. In fact peasants are reacting quite logically to the prices they are allowed to set, the opportunities available, and the structures being imposed on them—by going back to subsistence agriculture. Across the country, compulsory quota deliveries, proliferating taxes, and the collectivization of landholdings have discouraged production, throttled the peasantry, and increased vulnerability to drought. In many respects the Ethiopian famine of 1984–85 resembles that of 1921. No NEP followed in the aftermath, however, despite repeated warnings by Soviet experts worried by the grandiose objectives of the 10-year plan launched in September 1984, in the very midst of the period of famine. In a September 1985 report submitted to the Ethiopian authorities,[4] Soviet experts advocated new policies more favorable to peasant agriculture. But their recommendations—astonishingly close to those of the

---

[4] *Considerations on the Economic Policy of Ethiopia for the Next Five Years,* report prepared for the Ethiopian National Central Planning Committee.

World Bank—were not adopted by Ethiopian leaders. Far from reevaluating their strategy, they resolved instead on a program of shock therapy intended to radically transform rural Ethiopia. Taking advantage of a vulnerable society, its social institutions weakened by famine and the reliance on international aid as a source of supply, they undertook in record time to displace a large portion of the rural population for resettlement in new collective structures.[5] In the space of a few months, 600,000 starving persons were forcibly transferred from the north of the country to the south, and 3 million peasants were compelled to abandon their lands and gather in numerous villages, under the militia's surveillance.

This enormous eruption of activity, which has already claimed more than 100,000 victims and whose worst consequences are now plain to see, carries echoes of the rationale for the Great Leap Forward. There was the same refusal to be constrained by reality; the same headlong rush towards utopia; the same avalanche of grandiose objectives, with total collectivization seen as a shortcut to progress; and the same frenzy of transformation, in the belief that revolutionary enthusiasm could compensate for an absence of preparation, capital, or competence.

China: Fatal Utopia

Inaugurated in 1958 in an atmosphere of near hysteria, the Great Leap Forward envisaged that grain and steel production would double in one year and England would be outperformed in fifteen. The masses were entrusted with the execution of these miracles and duly shepherded by hundreds of thousands of cadres, sent into the field to instruct peasants in agriculture. Millions of people were uprooted from their lands in a deluge of massive hydraulic projects and mini-blast furnaces that proved in the end to be little more than fiascoes. The "metamorphosis of rivers and mountains" aggravated the flooding it was meant to prevent. The "battle for steel" prevented peasants from tending to their harvests—in sum, this dual industrial and agricultural leap was a triumph of absurdity. The frenzied obsession with productivity led to a collapse in production; the "victorious struggle against nature" led to unprecedented famine.

---

[5] François Jean, *Ethiopia, On the Proper Usage of Famine* (Médecins Sans Frontières, 1986).

All across China efforts to implement the slogan "more, faster, better, and cheaper" in every domain quickly devolved into general frenzy. Fearful of being denounced for right-wing tendencies, the more pragmatic cadres had no choice but to redouble their activism, throwing their regions into a vast competition for the status of model, or "Sputnik," province.[6] In this atmosphere of one-upmanship, goals proliferated, statistics soared, propaganda became panegyric, and reality itself was buried beneath triumphant official communiqués. Even as China collapsed into famine, senior and junior cadres brainwashed themselves and each other amid a profusion of eclipsed goals, "hydraulicized" provinces and "steel" villages ... It would take three years—and 28 million dead—for the veil of rhetoric finally to drop. In the final reckoning, political delirium weighed just as heavily on the scale as economic disaster; the catastrophe never would have reached such proportions if leaders had not been such prisoners of their own delusions.

In Ethiopia, at least, the response of the international community acted as a circuit breaker, obliging the regime to momentarily rein in its project for reconstructing the countryside. Population transfers were suspended in 1986–87 to dampen controversy sparked by the expulsion of Médecins Sans Frontières. As it turned out, the respite was only temporary. Population transfers are being resumed using the new famine as a pretext, and the intensified fighting in Eritrea and Tigre provides an alibi for expelling humanitarian organizations. "Pauses to consolidate" may alternate with phases of mobilization, but the regime's policies remain the same, sending the nation further into a spiral of famine and oppression.

---

[6] Jean-Luc Domenach, *The Origins of the Great Leap Forward: The Case of One Chinese Province*, trans. A.M. Berrett (Oxford: Westview Press 1995).

CHAPTER TWO

Ethiopia: A Political Famine

Originally published in *Politique Internationale*, No. 39, spring 1988, p.89-100

The respite, it turns out, was to be short-lived. Three years after the tragedy of 1984–85, famine once again threatens Ethiopia. Since September 1987, authorities there have been appealing for tons in relief supplies from the international community, evoking a grim sense of déjà vu ... Even in September 1984, the annual fall festivities marking the progress of the revolution were troubled by rumors—at the time suppressed—of widespread poverty in the countryside. From the creation of the Workers' Party in 1984 to the founding of the Democratic Republic in 1987, alarm bells of famine have attended every step in the construction of the New Ethiopia. This stubborn coincidence puts the customary alibi of drought in a questionable light. In 1984 Ethiopia was the emblematic image on our TV screens of an Africa in crisis, foreordained by a sort of destiny of climate to endless catastrophe. Now after a million dead, millions of refugees and displaced persons, millions of tons in food aid, and a new famine, questions have arisen. Drought can certainly provoke localized subsistence crises. But drought alone cannot fully explain tragedy on such a scale.

Drought leads to famine in Ethiopia because rural society is vulnerable to climate risk; it is vulnerable because it has been weakened by the conflict between Addis Ababa and guerilla movements and is being sacrificed on the altar of (unproductive) development and the "radiant future" to come.

This year, once again the map of zones menaced by famine covers precisely that of zones of conflict: Eritrea, Tigre, and North Wallo. In these regions especially sensitive to the vagaries of climate, the ravages of war and the army's atrocities have brought tragic consequences. Over the last 10 or even 20 years, the destruction of harvests and livestock, pillaging of villages and rural markets, and attacks on supply routes and convoys have hindered production, disrupted trade networks, and delayed crucial readjustments between zones of surplus and zones of shortage. The war that is ravaging Eritrea and Tigre is both a vehicle of famine and an obstacle to relief operations, a problem magnified by the fact that the rich agricultural regions of the central west can no longer meet the needs of the regions threatened. Ever since Colonel Mengistu took charge of the nation's fate, the food situation has deteriorated steadily. Revolutionary Ethiopia has become mired in chronic food shortage and growing dependence on Western aid. One-half of the relief supplies requested of the international community in September represented a structural deficit. If the trend that started in the 1970s continues, a "normal" year's needs may reach two million tons of grain in 1990.

These developments do not derive from a hostile climate, unforgiving soil, or rapid population growth, at least not for the most part. They are principally the result of regime policy. For 10 years nothing has been done to support the Ethiopian peasantry; scarce resources available for agriculture have been squandered in vain on state farms and cooperatives. Individual peasants, responsible for 95 percent of total production, have not merely been neglected but actively discouraged by pricing and distribution policies that verge on racketeering. Far from promoting conditions that would favor increased production, the regime is instead determined to find more ways of extorting surpluses. Across the country, compulsory quotas, increased taxes, and confiscations of grain reserves have discouraged production and throttled the peasantry, and increased its vulnerability to drought.

The Rulers' Rationale

These disastrous policies are most assuredly not the product of a collective death wish among Ethiopia's leadership. Rather they reflect very clear priorities: feeding the politically sensitive population of the capital, bankrolling a stronger state apparatus, and meeting the army's needs. They also reveal a deep contempt for traditional peasants, supposedly incapable of acting rationally. In truth, by going back to subsistence agriculture, the peasantry is reacting quite logically to the opportunities available, the prices they are allowed to set, and the structures being imposed on them … Paradoxically, this reaction only confirms the biases of the military men in power: even when freed from their "feudal-bourgeois" shackles, peasants remain mired in tradition, hostile to progress, incapable of perceiving "their" best interests. In the heroic struggle to enlighten the New Ethiopia, peasants are viewed as being in the way. According to Colonel Mengistu, "there is no alternative to peasant collectivization."[1] In this view, the only way to bring science and technology to the countryside is to reconfigure landholdings into massive agro-complexes; the only way to build discipline and productivity is by gathering peasants into large production units. More important, it is the only way to bring their production under control. Flawless logic; and it is ruthlessly applied. "Backward" peasants—individualist, potentially insurgent—must be rounded up, reeducated, and ultimately converted into model tractor operators. Colonel Mengistu's speeches echo Stalin's in their visions of a future Ethiopia crisscrossed by a network of machine and tractor stations, work brigades, and housing cooperatives.

The failure of state-owned farms doesn't seem to have threatened this splendid agenda. In Colonel Mengistu's view, if the collective sector is less productive than individual peasants, this is precisely because the latter have not yet been sufficiently collectivized. According to a circular argument only Ethiopia's leaders are able to parse, the logical remedy is to move quickly to increase the acreage of state farms and speed up the resettling of peasants into producers' cooperatives. Even the Soviets betrayed a certain anxiety when, in a September 1985 report to the Ethiopian authorities,[2] they emphasized the need to maintain the dynamism of small peasant farmers intact. Colonel Mengistu ignored their recommendations, opting instead for a headlong rush into massive population displacements and resettlements.

A Regime In Quest Of Funds

Ethiopia is probably the only African nation where a revolutionary rhetoric coincides with the actual execution of a radical project of social restructuring. It is also the only state that has prepared itself to reach this goal. In Ethiopia, with its ancient traditions of bureaucracy and state

---

[1] Report of the Central Committee of the Ethiopian Workers Party, April 8, 1985 (BBC—translated from Amharic).

[2] *Considerations on the Economic Policy of Ethiopia for the Next Five Years*, report prepared by Soviet experts under the direction of V.V. Sokolov for the Ethiopian National Committee for Central Planning.

dominance, the new regime has progressively acquired the tools it needs to control masses of its citizens. The regime's takeover began in 1978 with the repression of 20,000 peasants' associations; it was further consolidated in 1984 with the creation of a vanguard party of 30,000 cadres duly trained by the Soviets, and completed in 1987 when a people's democratic republic was established with a new constitution and redrawn territorial boundaries. Still, Colonel Mengistu's regime has neither the financial resources nor the margin of security it needs to radically transform the countryside at the cost of a breakdown in production. The regime expects those resources to come from Western nations.

The East and the West have long played nursemaid to Ethiopia in a specific division of labor familiar from other instances: the West provides budgetary support and increasing amounts of food aid, mainly in the form of donations; the Soviets deliver arms, gasoline, or materials for tractor facilities, mostly as loans or barter in exchange for staple foods.[3] In 1985, for example, the figure for arms purchases from the USSR was equal to total expenditures by Western governments on relief aid for victims of famine. While content with the resources their allies provide, Ethiopia's leaders realize there are limits to this economic aid.

Since the early 1980s the regime has actively sought Western support. A team from the International Labor Office was brought in to assess Ethiopia's needs in the hope that a favorable report from an international organization would draw donor attention. The project did not furnish the results anticipated: the commission's members—though carefully composed of experts sympathetic to the socialist alternative—were unsparing in their criticism. Highlighting the disastrous results of policies pursued and noting the leadership's firm resolve to continue on the same path, the commission simply advised it not to rely on Western aid.[4] And in fact, with the exception of (extensive) assistance provided in the context of emergency operations, Ethiopia is among the least favored African

---

[3] Still, on January 25, 1988, the Soviets did announce a contribution of 250,000 tons of grain, making them, with the United States, the chief donors. During the 1984–85 famine Soviet food aid was negligible (roughly 10,000 tons of rice).

[4] BIT, *Socialism from the Grassroots: Accumulation, Employment and Equity in Ethiopia* (Addis Ababa, 1982, unpublished).

governments in terms of development aid. Some find this objection-
able; confusing the cause and effect, they censure the West for keep
ing the country in poverty by denying it resources it needs to develop.
Unaccountably blind, these hardline advocates for injecting more
resources now propose that we finance the repression of rural areas—by
way of atonement! Still, how can they fail to see that aid without conditions serves only to insulate the regime from the disaster it is inflicting on
its people and … to supply it the means to carry on doing so? Clearly the
best support we could offer the Ethiopians would be to make aid conditional on a radical change in direction.

The Aid In Question
Donors are aware of all this and want reforms that offer hope of positive results in return for their support. How forcefully those wishes are
expressed varies greatly. The firmest position is that of the United States,
which provides humanitarian assistance alone. At the opposite pole, Italy
finances "Ethiopian-style development" without compunction, whether
from some larger strategy or mere impulse it is not clear. Between these
two poles, donors range from the World Bank, which demands reforms,
to the Swedish Agency for Development, which supports projects considered "neutral." In between is the European Economic Community (EEC),
which refrains from setting conditions and instead prefers to talk of a
"policy dialogue."

After five years of in-depth discussions the World Bank still awaits a change
in policy. During March 1986 meetings to allocate funds granted Ethiopia
under the third Lome Convention, the EEC secured promises. Doubtless
it would have been satisfied with promises alone; France and Great Britain
preferred to wait until these materialized. Even the Swedish, who operate in
a rapidly developing region, are beginning to think it no longer possible to
ignore the circumstances surrounding their projects. Since 1986, when they
registered their concerns on the resettling of peasants in new villages, the
ban on private commerce, and the introduction of cooperatives, they have
fallen in line with the World Bank's position and plan to withdraw by the
end of 1988 if no change is perceived by that date.

Still, negotiations have made progress; they focus, instructively, on the concept of quotas. It is clear the two parties do not share the same perspective: donors seek to stimulate production while Colonel Mengistu, his gaze lifted towards the radiant future to come, thinks to control it. His position was amply expressed in a 1981 speech: "When we planned our nation's development, it was with the strategic objectives of our revolution in mind …. Some people have forgotten that the sole foundation of our revolution is the ideology we represent. Some tend to overlook this point, mistaking economic reconstruction for an end in itself."[5]

The leadership's thinking is transparent, unless one resorts to an applied Kremlinology that sees "pragmatists" and "ideologues" struggling for the upper hand. Pragmatists do indeed exist, and their convictions are reinforced whenever donors show firmness. But until now there has been no concrete evidence to support the notion that any such movement towards liberalization—meaning a lesser degree of terror—might be taking place. None of the signals periodically emitted—causing analysts to wonder: NEP? or is collectivization being challenged?—have found the faintest echo in official speeches. In September 1987 Colonel Mengistu reemphasized that "[Our] efforts to build socialism cannot bear fruit in agriculture unless the private sector is replaced by a socialist sector."[6]

Yet all it took was Ethiopia's expressing a willingness to respect its commitments for the EEC straightaway to proclaim the coming release of 239 million ECUs promised under Lome III a "success."[7] The Ethiopian regime was known to be anxious to reach an accord with its financial backers, even if this required a tactical retreat on its part. European authorities were known to be impatient to speed the payout of funds allotted Ethiopia. Still, it is regrettable that in the end the "policy dialogue" yielded little more than technical measures with scant hope, for now, of actual implementation.

---

[5] Colin Legum, ed., *African Contemporary Records: 1981-1982* (New York: Africana Publishing Co., 1981).

[6] Blaine Harden, "Ethiopia Faces Famine Again, Requests Massive Food Relief," *The Washington Post*, September 14, 1987.

[7] Ethiopia is the first beneficiary to receive community aid under Lome III. Because the amount of aid was pre-set (primarily based on population and level of development), current discussions center on the utilization of funds.

The More Things Change ...

Caution is all the more in order now that population displacement and "villagization"[8] are once again on the agenda. In reality villagization never stopped. At most the pace was slowed to placate donors: from December 1985 to December 1987 more than six million peasants were forced to abandon their lands and resettle in new villages under the watch of the militia. Population displacements involving the forced transfer of 600,000 northern peasants towards the supposedly "fertile, virgin" south did have to be suspended, on the other hand, for a "pause to consolidate" amid controversy following the expulsion of Médecins Sans Frontières in December 1985.[9]

It would appear the time has come to move on to the next stage. In November 1987, even as Ethiopia issued repeated appeals for Western aid, its National Coordinating Committee for Villagization announced its new 1988 goals to cadres: three million peasants are to be resettled in new villages and 300,000 people are to be called on to begin training in the socialist mode of production on the new southern frontier. With curious inevitability, each crisis occasions a fresh acceleration of the process. Just as in 1984, when the "discovery" of famine was accompanied by brutally implemented population displacement and resettlement programs, so the new threat of famine is prompting a large-scale relaunching of operations. The timing is no coincidence. Famine in Ethiopia is more than second nature; it is a mode of governing. Though never desired by the leadership, famine has nonetheless allowed it to reach its goals more quickly. Famine provides the resources for the regime to effect profound change in a society of decaying institutions, to justify the upheaval taking place, and to obtain from the international community the tools it needs to transform the countryside.

---

[8] Population displacements and "villagization" are very different in their scale of activity: population displacements involve the transfer of peasants north to resettlement camps situated many hundreds of kilometers from the south. In contrast, "villagization" is a local operation in which populations that traditionally have lived in scattered settlements are resettled in new villages.

[9] Médecins Sans Frontières was expelled from Ethiopia for publicly denouncing the conditions in which population displacements were being carried out, which flouted principles the regime had established (voluntary participation, non-separation of families, the displaced were to be in a good state of health, etc.)

1984–1985: Booby-Trapped Aid

The experience of the last famine is enlightening in this regard. The regime obtained on an emergency basis the development aid it had previously been refused. What is worse, the famine could have been controlled and limited, as developments in Ethiopia and Kenya in 1983–84 demonstrate.[10] These two countries, relatively alike in their geographic configuration, agricultural potential, and rainfall conditions, were indeed both struck by a serious drought that led to similar food shortages. Yet Kenya emerged from this difficult period essentially unscathed, while Ethiopia descended into a disaster without precedent. The Kenyan "nonevent" attracted little notice, of course, and no one marveled at this very odd famine that would spare Kenya only to hit Ethiopia the harder. But there was no great feat in the Kenyan "miracle." Simple recognition of the threat early on, combined with the political will to avoid the catastrophe, were all that was needed. As a result the problem never developed into a crisis. It was treated as a priority by existing institutions; food supplies, imported from the first months of 1984, were regularly dispatched to villages via normal trade channels, and peasants were able to return to their fields with the coming of the first rains.

In Ethiopia, by contrast, sophisticated emergency warning systems, expert committees on natural disasters, and other extensive emergency response mechanisms could not compensate for months of dissembling and indifference. In fact, it took almost a year and tens of thousands of victims for the regime to finally acknowledge the "drought" and authorize journalists to film—under surveillance—crowds of starving people stranded at distribution centers. As we know, the images were deeply moving, prompting the largest relief operation ever. Kenya, on the other hand, was forgotten. It could not produce images of abandoned villages, massive migrations, masses of starving people, or emaciated children. While Kenya imported two-thirds of its needs, at great cost, Ethiopia hit the international-aid "jackpot." Not that it acted in deliberate manipulation: Ethiopian leaders were clearly too busy with preparations for the revolution's 10th anniversary

---

[10] John M. Cohen, "Role of Government in Combating Food Shortages," in *Drought and Hunger in Africa*, ed. M. Glantz (Cambridge, 1986).

celebrations to concern themselves with the famine or international public opinion! Nevertheless, the example highlights one of the paradoxes of aid; at times it means rewarding the most irresponsible or the most criminal of regimes, allowing them to cash in on the consequences of disastrous policies, pursue them with total impunity, and even accelerate a process that generates refugees, famines, and … more relief aid.

The problem is by no means a theoretical one. In 1984 and 1985 aid essentially financed population displacements and resettlements. It also made it possible to offset a drop in production the following year caused by this radical upheaval. By officially refusing support to these operations while turning a blind eye to the way aid was being used, donors have let themselves become ensnared in a deadly cycle. Whether by blindness or consent, they made it possible to finance the "great leap forward" mandated by Ethiopia's leadership; in so doing they condemned themselves to foot the bill for these social experiments indefinitely, in order to care for its victims. Thus assured of a comfortable safety net, Colonel Mengistu could redouble his efforts to "create a new constructive man for the new society"[11] free of concern for the economic impact. The human impact, however, was appalling. One hundred thousand people are dead who could have been saved had donors not resigned themselves, by their silence, to condoning violence, blackmail, and the diversion of relief aid. None of the principles solemnly proclaimed for the benefit of donors were ever respected.

Intoxicating Success

The regime has since acknowledged the most overt atrocities and denounced the overzealousness of local cadres. Likewise, Colonel Mengistu has offered to placate donors with the promise that future population displacements will be on a wholly voluntary basis. It is hardly astonishing that such declarations would be offered in appeasement. What does surprise is that they should continue to find a receptive audience, as we see nowadays in the responses of certain obliging analysts, eager to

---

[11] Fisseha Desta (Vice President of the Republic and of the Council of State, Workers Party politburo member), *Address to Last DERG Conference*, (trans. from Amharic by the BBC) September 3, 1987.

exonerate the leadership and circulate its alibis of individual misconduct. When the time came to relaunch the regime's program in the presence of invited journalists and donors, noble declarations and the smiles of departing first volunteers were quite enough to hearten certain observers, who are obviously impressed by "laudable efforts"[12] such as these to promote development. The military-industrial complex, identified with a hated imperialism, has now been replaced by a military-progressive complex that cultivates the image of vanguard liberators anxious to guide "a little people, impoverished but worthy" along the road of development.

In many ways the innocuous label "development"—a fig leaf for the most criminal of undertakings—has a truly numbing effect. Superficially benevolent intentions are supposed to excuse, a priori, some of the "regrettable" consequences of the struggle against dependence and underdevelopment. Yet, how is it possible not to see that the bizarre goals set for cadres—compelled to reach their quotas for deliveries, resettlement, villagization, and collectivization with forced enthusiasm—by their very nature lead to coercion and abuse? Clearly, these excesses are not so much the result of the particular tenacity of local authorities as they are the logical product of a system that seeks to lead an entire society on a forced march towards an absolute, compulsory Good.

This is not yet clear to some analysts, however, who continue to maintain that Ethiopia is only trying to apply solutions long prescribed by donors themselves. It is true that since 1973 the World Bank has endorsed limited population displacements to deal with problems in a few regions. However, its concern has been with soil conservation, not the reconfiguration of rural areas. Once again donors are mistaken as to the regime's intentions. But there is an ample supply of witness accounts that leave no doubt as to the operation's true objectives. Dawit Wolde Giorgis, longtime political analyst of the regime for financial donors, supplied a loose interpretation after his defection:[13] "The goal [of population displacements] is

---

[12] Statement by Professor Minkowski on his return from Ethiopia, AFP, January 20, 1988.

[13] Dawit Wolde Giorgis, head of the Ethiopian organization in charge of relief aid (RRC), defected in November 1985 during a tour of Western capitals. His successor as head of the RRC, Berhane Deresa, in turn sought refuge in the United States on June 6, 1986, during the United Nations' special session on Africa.

to create the nucleus of new collective farms ...; villagization has the same goal. Social control and mobilization is the only political process now taking place in Ethiopia."[14]

What to Do?

Western aid must be kept carefully separate from such a process. This is true for development aid, the intent of which surely is not to reinforce policies that condemn the country to an ongoing state of catastrophe. It is just as true for emergency aid intended to provide relief to the starving, not to fund a lunatic project of social transformation. Donors would be well advised to draw the reasonable conclusions, or else be trapped in a purely bureaucratic logic. Development aid should be suspended until these experiments are abandoned.

Emergency aid, however, is needed now more than ever. At a time when famine threatens millions of Ethiopians, it is vital to avoid another slaughter. Nevertheless, it must be with the assurance that this aid mobilized on the victims' behalf will not be deflected from its target. This means monitoring its use and ensuring that it reaches the hungry.

At present these two imperatives are jeopardized by the war. Guerilla forces are achieving important victories in Eritrea and Tigre, and a counteroffensive is being readied. The regime recently compelled the departure of NGOs working in the north of the country, and the renewed outbreak of fighting is paralyzing relief operations. Food aid unloaded at Ethiopian ports can no longer be directed to zones threatened by famine. Airlifts are inadequate; the distribution of supplies, henceforth under government control, will affect only provincial capitals, while rural areas remain out of reach of international aid. With the forced exit of humanitarian organizations, millions of peasants are now stranded, with no one to witness, between war and famine.

---

[14] See "Let Them Eat Dust," *African Events III*, August 1987.

CHAPTER THREE

North Korea: A Famine Regime

Originally published in *Esprit*, February 1999

In the spring of 1995, several months after the end of a crisis triggered by Pyongyang's threatened withdrawal from the nuclear nonproliferation treaty, North Korea was back in the headlines with an appeal for food aid. A disbelieving world thus learned that this tightly sealed nation, on the brink of possessing a nuclear weapon and long-range missiles, was also a nation drained dry, incapable of feeding its people and dependent on international aid for survival. North Korea has been on international life support for four years now. The food emergency, first characterized by officials first as the result of flooding in 1995–96, then of drought in 1997, set in motion one of the largest food aid programs financed by the international community in the past decade.

For the past four years, the rare humanitarian organizations authorized to travel in North Korea have speculated about the scale of the crisis. Some speak of an acute food shortage; others depict a situation of famine that, depending on estimates, would have caused between many hundreds of thousands and more than three million deaths over recent years. The degree of uncertainty is a clear consequence of the nation's impenetrable facade. The North Korean regime has now lifted a corner of the veil, of course, in its request for international aid, but it continues to conceal the gravity of the situation. In this country, isolated from the world and wrapped in a siege mentality, all economic and social data—even hospital patient registers—are considered state secrets. Moreover, the few humanitarian organizations present in the country are subject to strict monitoring and are unable to freely evaluate the situation. They may on occasion see cases of acute malnutrition, but they can only observe what the regime allows to be seen.

Beneath such difficulties of assessment, however, speculations about the dimensions of the crisis reveal a deeper flaw in our perception of the process of famine in North Korea.

An Atypical Famine

Famine may be one of the most neglected aspects of contemporary history. Compared to war, deeply rooted in the Western imagination as the embodiment of adversity, famine touches our awareness only sporadically. Images of starving children flash around the world on TV screens, only to vanish in the onrush of the news cycle. In this awkward encounter with uttermost distress, analysis of any kind seems unnecessary. With thousands of studies devoted to wars and conflict it would be hard to list even a small number of books on famines; most are familiar only to specialists. But our ignorance exacts a heavy toll; it blinds us to the lessons of history, condemning us not to see, or else not to understand, the famines of the present day. The famines of 25 years ago materialized under the incredulous gaze of TV-watchers equipped, so to speak, with high-powered binocuars for the occasion. Since that time, with some interval between, events in Ethiopia have again opened our eyes to the issue.[1] But the notion that modern famines frequently are the result of the combined effects of drought and war, while perfectly accurate, does not exhaust the question. While continual references to "hunger as a weapon" lock our attention on nations in conflict, other famines may remain hidden from view. "The hand of fate" ... the "ravages of war" ... famine eludes our understanding in fashionable clichés such as these. For several years now, our iconic images of famine have come from Somalia or Sudan. By this yardstick there could be no famine in North Korea, because it cannot furnish the images we instinctively associate with such a tragedy. What strange sort of famine could this be, with no massive migrations or starving hordes crowding distribution centers, no de-structuring of society, no destabilization of political authority?

---

[1] François Jean, *Ethiopie, du Bon Usage de la Famine* [Ethiopia: On the Proper Usage of Famine] (Médecins Sans Frontières, 1986).

Yet circumstances such as these are not unprecedented. Quite the contrary—they are features shared by the worst famines of this century. In Ukraine in 1933, six million people perished silently in the breadbasket of Eastern Europe, hermetically sealed off by cordons of militia.[2] Similarly, famine took the lives of 30 million people in the Chinese countryside between 1959 and 1961, before migrations from starving villages towards the cities forced Mao to reign in the ideological frenzy of the Great Leap Forward.[3] In both cases strict control over information and the population enabled authorities to firmly reassure an international public that otherwise might have been agitated by refugee accounts. After viewing productions skillfully orchestrated for their benefit, an Édouard Herriot in Ukraine or a François Mitterand in China felt entitled to deny any famine existed at all. Indeed, it was necessary to wait until the aftermath of the Second World War and its flood of refugees, as well as de-Stalinization and the half truths it uncovered, for the slaughter in Ukraine to appear in its fullest dimensions. In like manner, the most prescient fears of China watchers concerning the toll of the 1959–61 famine would not be confirmed until 20 years later, when previously unpublished demographic data became available. North Korea is not the first country to experience a famine amidst genuine skepticism abroad. If not for refugee accounts and questions raised by those close to the reality in North Korea, one could easily doubt whether anyone is dying of hunger at all in this kingdom of self-reliance.

But comparisons to Ukraine in the 1930s or China during the Great Leap Forward can also be misleading. Beneath surface similarities, North Korea's famine has features that distinguish it from every other modern famine.

In contrast with most of the famines of the 20th century, North Korea's is not associated with a situation of conflict. North Korea is, of course, still technically at war with the United Nations, but a peace agreement was reached in 1953 and the famine is not, as in Somalia or Sudan, the end result of a conflict and its ensuing train of devastation. This suspended state of hostilities is a key contributing factor in the deteriorating situation,

---

[2] Robert Conquest, *The Harvest of Sorrow* (Oxford University Press, 1986).

[3] Jasper Becker, *Hungry Ghosts,* John Murray (1996).

however, because it has a deep impact on the setting of priorities and the allocation of resources. North Korea devotes more than a quarter of its GDP to defense, maintains an army of over one million men, and has for 40 years run an economy—with tunnels filled with strategic stocks and specialized steelworks facilities—that is inefficient but geared nonetheless towards reunifying the nation by military means. A perpetual state of mobilization for imminent conflict is intrinsic to the regime's legitimacy. It is as if North Korea could not exist if it were not encircled by a hostile world. This isolationism is a key element of the country's present impasse.

The North Korean famine is also dissimilar to famines under other communist regimes in that it is not the consequence of a crash project of social transformation. The acute food shortages that arose in Mongolia at the beginning of the 1930s, in Vietnam from 1955 to 1956, or in Cambodia from 1977 to 1979—and particularly the widespread famines that ravaged Ukraine, Kazakhstan, and China—were the direct result of radical changes in landholding patterns and sharply increased state levies on the peasantry.[4] And the Ukrainian tragedy was the crowning phase of a policy of collectivization and requisition, aimed at eliminating both peasants and Ukrainians and subjugating survivors to state and party authority once and for all. The calamity of the 1959–61 famine, which not only struck every corner of China but did so for an unprecedented three years running, was directly linked to the frenzied obsession with productivity and the ideological one-upmanship characteristic of the Great Leap Forward. Nothing at all similar took place in North Korea, where famine has occurred under a stable regime, firmly in power for a half century, which has not embarked on any radical change of course in recent years. But the fact that the current crisis cannot be traced to recent policy decisions does not make the search for solutions any easier. The problem is a structural one.

Finally, and in contrast to other famines of this century—especially those of the USSR and China, which hit primarily rural societies—North Korea's famine has occurred in a country with a majority urban population and an

---

[4] François Jean, "Famine et Idéologie" [Famine and Ideology], *Commentaire*, vol. 11, no. 42 (summer 1988).

economy based principally on heavy industry.[5] This hampers the population's ability to fall back on a subsistence livelihood as well as the regime's capacity to extract from the countryside the resources urban dwellers need for survival. City dwellers cannot plant rice on their balconies; they have been wholly dependent on government-distributed resources (food, clothing, etc.) for three generations. But if the state tries to wring from peasants more than they can produce, it risks triggering famine and jeopardizing future harvests. There are no easy answers in such a situation. The problem is systemic; it is a product of deficiencies in the now bankrupt North Korean economy.

Chronic Scarcity

Any attempt to analyze the North Korean situation is frustrated from the outset by a lack of data. Since the 1960s the country has been under a statistical blackout unrivalled in contemporary history; by comparison Enver Hoxha's Albania would have passed for a paradigm of transparency. Moreover, the majority of analysts are forced to work from data published by the Bank of Korea based on estimates by information services and filtered politically by the government in Seoul. The more diligent observers try to interpret economic developments in North Korea by careful analysis of its foreign trade data, which they seek to reconstruct from information published by major trade partners.[6]

In the agricultural sector, as well, this cult of secrecy has produced long statistical gaps during the 1960s, the early 1970s, and the end of the 1990s. The rare data published on the occasion of New Year's addresses or at the end of seven-year plans more closely resembled paeans to the march of socialist agriculture—until the sheer magnitude of economic stagnation, made worse when Eastern-bloc regimes suspended aid, forced the regime to lift a corner of the veil to reveal its agricultural shortages as part of its appeal for international aid. Grain production thus appears to

---

[5] Nicholas Eberstadt, "North Korea as an Economy under Multiple Severe Stresses: Analogies and Lessons from Past and Recent Historical Experience," *Communist Economies & Economic Transformation*, vol. 9, no. 2 (1997).

[6] Nicholas Eberstadt, "The DPRK's international trade in capital goods, 1970-1995: Data from 'Mirror Statistics,'" *The Journal of East Asian Affairs*, vol. XII, no 1 (winter/spring 1998).

have soared—from 1.9 million tons in 1946 to 4.8 million tons in 1961, 7 million tons in 1974, and 10 million tons in 1984 and 1995—before collapsing to 3.76 million tons in 1995, the year of the first request for international aid.[7]

This pattern prompts two observations and poses a question. The first observation is that the regime's rhetoric has been not altogether divorced from reality: it is consistent with the bell curve of the nation's economic development. Initial successes based on an extensive mobilization of resources were followed by more or less rapid setbacks, due to autarchic policies and structural obstacles. The second observation is that the bell was probably flatter than indicated, beginning its downward curve in the second half of the 1980s. Clearly this statistical series is more a product of political propaganda than of economic data. And, in North Korea, propaganda is ubiquitous to the point that it actually furnishes keys to interpretation: the heavy-handed recycling of the old '60s slogan "Rice = Socialism" (to become "Rice = Communism" 20 years later), along with repeated promises of Korean chicken-in-a-pot (soup with meat and rice) in New Year's addresses, as well as the "Let's eat just two meals a day" campaign—launched in the midst of an otherwise abundant period statistically—have fueled doubts since the early 1990s concerning the successes proclaimed in official addresses.

The difficulty lies in knowing whether this exaggeration is principally meant for foreign consumption or is part of a process of self-induced brainwashing. Here, again, the sermons of the Great Leader can at times provide surprising insight into the reality behind the one-upmanship, whereby senior and junior cadres alike brainwash themselves and each other in a profusion of obliterated targets, exceeded quotas, and record harvests. In a 1974 address to agricultural cadres, Kim Il Sung castigated cooperative farm authorities for the exaggerations in their reports.[8] In

---

[7] Philip Wonhyuk Lim, "North Korea Food Crisis," *Korea and World Affairs*, vol. 21 (winter 1997); Kim Woon Keun, "The Food Crisis in North Korea: Background and Prospects," *East Asian Review*, vol. VIII, no. 4 (winter 1996).

[8] March 31, 1975 address to agricultural officials in South Pyongyang province, in Kim Il Sung, *Jojakjib* [Works], vol. 30 (1987), quoted in Hy-Sang Lee, "Supply and Demand for Grains in North Korea," *Korea and World Affairs* (1994).

North Korea, status and social standing depend on the ability to fill production quotas set at the next level up. There is an inherent tendency in such a system to exaggerate at each level—still more so in a climate of endless mobilization campaigns. Despite, or indeed because of this activist atmosphere and this triumphal obsession with productivity, it is doubtful whether North Korea ever produced 10 million tons of grain; estimates for the end of the 1980s vary between 5 and 7 million tons and, for the beginning of the 1990s, between 4 and 5 million tons.[9]

Given what is known about the country's demographic development and the (Spartan) rations allocated to the population by the state, there is every reason to believe that by the early 1990s agricultural production could no longer meet the needs of the population as the regime defined them. It appears the deterioration was rapid. In 1991 the shortage was probably already on the order of millions of tons. It then grew steadily deeper, reaching an average of more than two million tons per year around the mid-1990s, which is when the appeal for international aid went out. At first rations were reduced; later the regime drew on reserves built up as a consequence of Kim Il Sung's mania for stockpiling resources in the event of imminent war. Next, it extended its practice of begging to include "imperialist" countries and requested international aid. Taking this attempt to reconstruct events a bit further, it would appear that, in any case, the food problem in North Korea began well before the floods of 1995. It accumulated over time, the product of policies implemented over a 50-year period.

A Bankrupt Economy

The land in North Korea is poorly suited to agriculture. A mountainous country situated in the northern latitudes, it has a brief agricultural season and only 2 million hectares of arable land, of which 1.5 million is used for grains—half for rice and half for corn since collectivization began. These natural limitations are compounded by the characteristic flaws of planned, collective-agriculture economies: poor resource allocation, an inefficient system of distribution, and, most of all, the lack of any

---

[9] Heather Smith, "North Korea: How Much Reform and Whose Characteristics?" *Brookings Discussion Papers*, no. 133 (July 1997).

structure of incentives for peasants, who from 1958 on have been settled on government farms and in production cooperatives. To compensate for the lack of economic incentives the regime relies on ideological mobilization and science-based agricultural methods.

Though neither the Ch'llima Movement[10] at the close of the 1950s nor the "Three Revolutions Teams"[11] introduced in the countryside since 1973 seem to have generated the surge of frenzied enthusiasm or the profound radicalization of either the Great Leap Forward or the Cultural Revolution in China, North Koreans have for the past half century been subject to an ideological mobilization practically unrivaled in intensity over such a lengthy period. Since the introduction in the 1960s of the "Chongsanri" method, which advocates the intensive, individual indoctrination of peasants by local cadres, the goal has been to boost agricultural production and achieve self-reliance in food production, transforming individualist, "backward" peasants "devoid of social consciousness" into model workers. The theoretical framework for these three revolutions—ideological, technological, and cultural—is set forth in Kim Il Sung's 1964 "Rural Theses." Their practical application proceeds from ad hoc suggestions distilled from the Great Leader himself in the course of his countless field visits.

The essence of the "eternal" president's all-encompassing wisdom is contained in this canon of teachings—the "Juche" farming method"; it is an elementary primer of scientism and Stakhanovism. Kim Il Sung was an apostle of a practice derived from Lyssenko's theories, which achieved a popularity in the China of the Great Leap Forward as far-reaching as the disaster that later ensued. On the theory that plants of the same species cannot be in class conflict, and therefore have no reason to struggle amongst themselves for light or nutrients, members of agricultural cooperatives were forced to use high-density planting. Likewise, the Great Leader has become an advocate of transplanting corn—a worthwhile innovation to be sure in this country of long, severe winters, but one that

---

[10] "Flying Horse": the North Korean version of the Great Leap Forward.

[11] This movement, similar to China's Cultural Revolution, sought to intensify revolutionary ardor and shake up bureaucracy by sending students and cadres out into the field. Its initiation in 1973 under the supervision of Kim Jong-il marked the accession of Kim Il Sung's son as the Great Leader's designated successor.

requires sending manpower into the countryside at key points during the agricultural calendar. No surprise, then, that North Korea should be the only practitioner of this farming method in the world, which relies on intensive mobilization of the labor force. The nation is unrivaled in this respect, with a labor force participation of over 70 percent, equal to China's at the end of the Maoist era. Lastly, Kim Il Sung's fascination for terrace farming and obsession with expanding arable land area have resulted in enormous terracing projects—but also in mountain deforestation, an important factor in the country's extreme vulnerability to flooding.

Apart from the consequences of deforestation, however, the Great Leader's directives have not in themselves led the country to ruin. On the contrary, North Korea appears to have avoided most of the failures other communist regimes have encountered in the early stages of their race to socialist agriculture. From what we know, the lightning collectivization of the countryside between 1954 and 1958 amidst the ruins of the Korean War did not lead to the collapse of the rural economy, as it did in the USSR and Vietnam. North Korea also appears to have been spared the eruptions of frenzied activity characteristic of Mao's China, where it was believed revolutionary fervor could compensate for an absence of preparation, competence, or capital. North Korea seems to have managed its progress towards a more scientific agriculture without notable deviation, via a "technological revolution" based on the four cornerstones of irrigation, electrification, mechanization, and chemicalization.

This quest for self-reliance, through modernization of the countryside and industrialized agriculture, was conducted in very nearly "classic" form: a succession of seven-year plans, a torrent of electrified villages and irrigated land, and tons of grains per hectare and tractors per hundreds of hectares. But early successes were soon frustrated by the rigidities of a highly centralized economy in which all investment decisions are dictated by the leadership. In a system where the Great Leader literally has a hand in everything—from decisions to replace grain factory compressors to whether or not to develop a given type of improved seed or a given sophisticated technology for coal gasification—resource-allocation decisions must follow a Byzantine course of visits to factories or cooperatives.

Moreover, the straitjacket of self-reliance has led to the manipulation of scarce resources as well as endless trade-offs between either industry and agriculture or the economy and the army, depending on the circumstances: first, growth and militarization in the 1960s and 1970s, then stagnation in the 1980s, and finally the recent collapse. A tractor factory might have switched to producing tanks at the end of the 1960s, then tractors for export at the end of the 1970s, and then, most likely, nothing but spare parts or scrap metal.

The progress of this industrial agriculture, which consumes copious amounts of inputs—mainly in the form of energy—for fertilizer factories, pumping stations, or agricultural machinery, is closely linked to other developments in the national economy. In a modern, complex economy—and North Korea's economy is certainly that—problems encountered in one sector have repercussions on economic activity as a whole. Agricultural development was very soon brought up short when the North Korean economy could not generate enough foreign currency from exports to buy raw materials, as well as equipment and the energy needed to run it. All through the 1980s concessionary trade with the Soviet bloc camouflaged the weaknesses inherent in this economic autarchy. The mirage of North Korean self-reliance evaporated when preferential trading terms lost support and the USSR itself finally fell apart. Between 1989 and 1992 oil imports from the USSR plunged from 500,000 tons to 30,000 tons.

The end of Eastern-bloc aid destabilized industry, transportation, and, in a sort of vicious circle of consequences, the entire economy of the nation, which was now unable to generate sufficient wealth to import the products it required to function and sustain the population. The food crisis gripping North Korea cannot in the end be traced to its agricultural sector, which despite inhospitable policies has performed fairly well given a natural environment little conducive to self-reliance. In the final analysis, the food crisis is the outgrowth of an energy crisis and, above all else, a scarcity of foreign currency.

When Food Self-Reliance Leads to Famine

An analysis of North Korea's foreign trade confirms how precarious the situation has always been, as well as its recent deterioration. In a system that deems foreign trade a necessary evil, foreign trade volume has steadily dwindled, until in 1994 it represented an absurdly narrow share—the smallest in the world—of about 10 percent of the estimated GDP.[12] Furthermore, this trade centers on a small number of partners, a reflection of the country's isolation, of course, but also its formidable capacity to extract unheard-of commercial terms of the kind that discourage potential exporters. The regime is past master in the art of squeezing the resources it needs for its survival out of friends (USSR, China) and even enemies (Japan, South Korea, the United States). In the 1960s Kim Il Sung skillfully exploited the Sino-Soviet split to raise the ante. In the 1970s he then turned to the West for about as long as it took to bounce a check, before securing concessionary trade terms from the Soviet Union in the 1980s. In spite of this unique form of trade, closer to de facto aid, North Korea has long recorded sizable, chronic trade deficits. It can no longer offset either Chinese exports at concessionary prices, or politically-motivated cheap South Korean imports, or even money transfers from Koreans in Japan, which have dropped sharply over recent years.[13] North Korea has accumulated over $10 billion in foreign debt, equal to 50 percent of its estimated GDP and is utterly without credit worthiness internationally. From 1972 to 1995 the trade deficit was close to half a billion dollars per year on average.

Upon closer examination of this chronic foreign trade deficit, the food sector offers a surprising picture. Between 1972 and 1995 food was the only sector with a trade balance: North Korea regularly secured surpluses—even in 1995, the year it first requested international aid. Given the general characteristics of North Korean foreign trade displays, such a marked contrast over such a long period is likely no accident; it derives from deliberate policy. Trade in food products seems subject to a rigid accounting concept of self-reliance—as if North Korean authorities have been under instructions not to spend more than they earn in food trade. If this interpretation is valid, then North Korea has made a clear political

---

[12] Young Namkoong, "Trends and Prospects of the North Korean Economy," *Korea and World Affairs*, vol. 20, no. 2 (summer 1996).

[13] These transfers, long estimated at several hundred million dollars per year, now represent little more than a few tens of millions of dollars per year, in all likelihood. See especially, Shim Jae Hoon, "Disillusioned Donors," *Far Eastern Economic Review* (December 4, 1997).

choice: not to use its precious foreign currency to purchase grain on the world market, even in bad years.

As part of this general policy of self-reliance, the regime has practiced an endless "arbitrage" between expensive exports and cheap imports in an effort to offset the growing food shortage. The pattern of food trade clearly indicates deteriorating circumstances in the course of the last 20 years; grain represented no more than 1 percent of food-product exports during the 1990s, compared to 70 percent in the 1970s. Over the years, regime officials appear to have tried to secure the maximum nutritive value in exchange for whatever they had left to sell in the food category.[14] They traded rice, with a high market value, for wheat flour (30 percent cheaper) during the 1970s. Then in the 1980s they traded rice for imports at concessionary prices to offset a growing quantitative shortage. Later there was no corn left to export, not even to obtain poor-quality corn ... Now North Korea sells mushrooms and seafood to Japan, at very high prices, to buy biscuits or cognac[15] for the governing elites and cheap grain for the rest of the population.

But the drying up of preferential trade terms in the mid-1990s brought an end to this "caloric arbitrage"—which appears to have been the foreign counterpart of domestic rationing. Although North Korea managed to acquire an average of over a half million tons of grain per year on the world market from the mid-1980s on—perhaps even starting in the 1960s if one accepts some of Kim Il Sung's assertions[16]—this subsidized self-reliance would be abruptly undercut by mounting impatience in China, North Korea's chief supplier of grain in the early 1990s. Weary of trade with North Korea at concessionary prices that amounted to de facto aid, China finally made its displeasure felt, after repeated warnings, by tem-

---

[14] Nicholas Eberstadt, "Food, Energy and Transport Equipment in the DPRK Economy: Some Indications from 'Mirror Statistics,'" *Asian Survey* (March 1998).

[15] In 1996, in the midst of famine, imports of French cognac and Armagnac increased by 780 percent compared to 1995.

[16] Hy-Sang Lee, "Supply and Demand for Grains in North Korea", op. cit.

porarily cutting off the flow.[17] The subsequent collapse of Chinese grain exports, from 800,000 tons to 300,000 in 1994, was probably what precipitated the recent crisis—months before the summer floods of 1995. North Korea's sudden incapacity to offset its structural food shortage with purchases of cheap grain triggered the mechanisms of international aid. In spite of the magnitude of the problem, North Korea remained straitjacketed in self-reliance: it refrained from buying the food it needed to feed its population on the world market and once again secured a trade surplus in food products in 1995. After drawing on its stockpiles of reserves throughout 1994, Pyongyang sent out an initial appeal for aid in the spring of 1995; South Korea and Japan responded generously. After the "natural disaster" in the fall of that same year, the United Nations became involved, launching one of the largest food aid programs of the past decade.

A Policy of Engagement ...

North Korea has been dependent on international aid for four years now. The regime has adapted itself quite well; after years of poor-quality grains, it is once again importing rice, and in large volumes. Foreign food trade is still in balance and, now that free imports have taken the place of imports at concessionary prices, the regime can still brandish the banner of food self-reliance ... Likewise, through nuclear blackmail Pyongyang was able to obtain two light-water reactor stations in October 1994 and, as they awaited activation, 500,000 tons of oil per year that would conveniently offset the loss of Soviet imports. Again, acknowledging its "agricultural troubles" enabled North Korea to receive sizeable amounts of aid to replace— or rather to augment, since Beijing had resumed its program in the

---

[17] China's decision seems to have been based on the desire, voiced by Beijing since the start of the decade and made official in 1993, to normalize bilateral trade, using dollars and at world-market prices. This may have been triggered, if official explanations are to be believed, by the poor harvests recorded in 1993 in the northeastern provinces bordering North Korea, due to a cold snap. But primarily it reflects Beijing's annoyance with a regime eager to promote propaganda against "revisionists" and other "traitors to the cause of socialism" or quite prepared to play the nuclear card—at the risk of unleashing an arms race likely to upset the balance of power in the region—in order to fashion itself as a negotiating counterpart to the United States. In any event, China very quickly gauged the possible repercussions of such a restrictive policy (i.e., the refugee camps hastily set up in border areas) and in 1995 returned to supplying grains at concessionary prices.

meantime—Chinese exports on preferential trading terms. Unprecedented though this avowal of failure may have been, it is no radical departure from past form. It is consistent with the longstanding practices of a regime that is past master of the tactical arts of unpredictable behavior. From nuclear threats to floods, from missile experimentation to famine, North Korea has continually exploited its nuisance capacity—be it as threat or as vulnerable victim, on the verge of exploding or imploding—to wring the resources it needs to survive from its friends and now its enemies.

The countries concerned have readily responded to this appeal for aid, showering ever increasing quantities of food aid on Pyongyang over the last four years. The chief impulse for this involvement is fear of a North Korean implosion. For, while each of these nations looks forward to the imminent end of this totalitarian system, they dread a sudden collapse. Their analyses are shaped by fears of instability and the spread of refugees, of political uncertainty and its strategic implications, and of the economic consequences of reunifying the Koreas. This is particularly so in South Korea, where the costs of German reunification were studied with extra concern because the demographic comparisons and economic gaps are more unfavorable, by far, in the Korean case. Seoul, Beijing, Washington, and Tokyo dread the scenario of an abrupt North Korean collapse and an "emergency reunification." For different reasons, therefore, each of these countries has pursued a policy of "constructive engagement" aimed at preserving stability on the peninsula and nurturing developments likely to facilitate a soft reunification of the two Koreas. Ex-South Korean president Kim Young Sam, comparing North Korea to an airplane rapidly losing altitude, has said the goal is to avert a crash and encourage a soft landing.

International engagement bases itself on the assumption that the current crisis presages the regime's imminent collapse. This view is debatable, even without making the sort of prognostications that enthralled many analysts at the time of Kim Il Sung's death in 1994. True, there is no lack of historical examples to show that serious economic troubles can lead to political upheaval. But no plausible theory exists to support a link between economic collapse and political change, particularly in totalitarian countries. The examples of the Soviet Union and China prove the contrary: that, far from weakening a regime, famine can contribute to the process of consolidating power. This is obviously not the case in North Korea, where famine has indeed occurred under a mature, no doubt enfeebled regime but also a stable one securely in power for a half century. The fact that we have so little data on the situation amply demonstrates, if that were necessary, the tight hold the government has over society and the absence of any forum for expression, let alone dissent, open to the population. Apart from the lack of data, however, the question is whether donor countries and entities truly understand how the regime is presently reacting to the crisis and managing it.

Betting on a soft landing assumes that, confronted with this economic impasse, it would be in the interest of North Korean leaders to implement the reforms needed to get the economy started again and that, in the short term, it would be in the regime's interests to feed the neediest in order to avoid population displacements and expressions of discontent— even revolt. In sum, the countries involved are proceeding on the theory that their notion of avoiding a crisis through a gradual opening up of society is consistent with the North Korean regime's priorities, if only because of a mutual concern over stability. The second assumption underpinning this policy of engagement is that international aid might encourage a dialogue over exactly what kind of political reforms the international community would be able to support during a transitional phase that would ease the system's gradual evolution.

For the North Korean regime, as well, the current situation is deeply ambiguous. For, while it has once again demonstrated its unrivaled capacity for obtaining the means of its survival from abroad, the cutoff of aid from Eastern-bloc countries did cause the leadership to turn to the "imperialist" nations. This innovation in its tradition of extortion poses a genuine challenge to a reclusive regime that keeps its people in complete isolation and draws legitimacy from how it deals with the hostile, squalid world outside. Any prospects for reform should be assessed in that light. Though it is quite likely that some North Korean leaders are at least conceptually aware of what reforms are needed to escape their predicament, they do not appear ready to run the political risks involved. Just as Seoul attentively followed the German reunification process, Pyongyang, too, watched—first in perplexity, then in horror—as the reform process in the

Eastern-bloc countries led to the breakup of the Soviet Union and the events in Tiananmen Square. The lessons they derived were all the more pointed given the very narrow margin for error in this divided country; any loss of control would lead not only to the fall of the regime but the disappearance of North Korea via absorption. In such a context, a posture of isolation and defiance towards the outside world is believed to be vital for the system's survival. The regime's primacy rests on ideology, and there is no reason to believe it will commit to reforms that might weaken its control over society.

... And "Humanitarian Aid"

International aid to North Korea has chiefly taken the form of emergency humanitarian relief, for two reasons: first, because it came in response to an appeal from North Korean authorities formulated in those terms. Officially, international assistance was meant to ease the impact of the flooding in 1995–96 and, later, the 1997 drought. And allusions to the natural disasters in North Korea have indeed become somewhat of a regular feature in United Nations reports. Bureaucrats at the international organization are doubtless not fooled by this rhetoric of climate-inspired famine, essentially generated by diplomatic considerations. Still, one can't help being struck by the remarkable similarities between regime propaganda and the stilted language of the United Nations—there is the sense, at times, that certain officials have been convinced by their own rhetoric. The second reason is that the humanitarian label enables donor countries to sweep aside any domestic reluctance to support the North Korean regime. In Washington, particularly, Reagan's doctrine that "a starving child knows no politics," declared during the 1984–85 Ethiopian famine, made it possible to secure the support of a Congress hostile to any form of aid to this communist country, still technically at war with the United States. In South Korea as well, humanitarian concerns cleared the path—after much hesitation—for aid to the other Korea, until the election of Kim Dae Jung and the introduction of a policy of engagement—the "sunshine policy"—provided a more favorable climate for initiatives towards the North.

Humanitarian aid has thus become a key element in diplomatic maneuverings between North Korea and the "international community," particularly in the context of multilateral talks between Pyongyang, Seoul, Washington, and Beijing to reduce tensions on the peninsula and work towards the possible signing of a peace treaty, 45 years after the truce accord of Panmunjom. Though it denies it, the United States uses humanitarian aid as a carrot and stick to bring North Korea to the negotiating table and make concessions, as demonstrated yet again by the release in October 1998 of 30,000 tons of food aid just prior to the renewal of talks. Pyongyang, on the other hand, tries to raise the ante by making the delivery of ever increasing quantities of food, or more recently grain, a precondition for joining the negotiations.

Though international aid is first and foremost a policy instrument, humanitarian concerns are not, for that reason, entirely absent. All the participants hope aid will ease the plight of the neediest groups. Faced with a closed nation in a state of paranoid relations with the outside world, donor countries have encouraged UN agencies and NGOs to intervene so as to ensure that aid to the "flood victims" truly reaches those for whom it is intended and is not used by the regime as an instrument of power or to feed the army. Furthermore, donor countries are hoping that an enhanced international presence, together with more and more mutual contact on the ground, will foster a climate of confidence and inspire a growing openness in the country. Pyongyang, on the other hand, sees these same humanitarian organizations as a collective Trojan horse and fears that they will have a "spiritually polluting" effect or weaken its control over society. While the regime has been obliged to accept the presence of a dozen humanitarian organizations in order to obtain aid, it goes to great lengths to limit their freedom of action.

North Korea is a dramatic example of delivering aid under murky conditions; the few humanitarian organizations authorized to work in the country are unable to determine the extent of the famine and are therefore reduced to distributing aid blindly. Despite every effort, the organizations present in the country since 1996 have never been able to establish two core principles of humanitarian action: assessing needs with complete independence and freely monitoring the distribution of aid. As a result they cannot guarantee humanitarian aid is truly reaching starving groups. They have been reduced to managing what is, in effect, economic aid to

North Korea. Certainly the issues of needs assessment and monitoring distribution are of major concern to the international community, but there is still little pressure exerted, perhaps because donor countries view humanitarian aid merely as an instrument to further the policy of engagement. Pyongyang understands this full well; it reacts virulently against even the mildest attempts to monitor food distribution. In January 1996 the Ministry of Foreign Affairs stated, "If biased interests continue to impede relief to North Korea by politicizing humanitarian issues, we will do without international aid."

Concealed Famine

This attitude is a key factor in North Korea's famine, which arose out of a breakneck pursuit of total self-reliance. Likewise, refusal to allow access of any kind allowed the famine to spread. There is no doubt that with better access to information and a quicker response, North Korea could have averted the famine. No matter where it hits, famine cannot spread without the aid of indifference or deliberate concealment.[18] In North Korea, as previously in the USSR or China, no one can say exactly to what extent the manipulation of information kept residents of the capital and its ruling elites in the dark as to the magnitude of the problem. Word of the famine doubtless now circulates in North Korea, along with reports of China's comparative affluence—this is a new and crucial development in a mobilized society isolated from the world such as this. But, if cadres do understand the seriousness of the situation, they will not speak frankly about it; they are creatures of the system's success. And international organizations, acting in response to the narrative of natural disaster, observe cases of acute malnutrition but are unable to identify which groups are threatened. A few manage, nevertheless, to experience some portion of the reality first hand but dare not speak out for fear of losing access to the country. A virtual smokescreen is thus created that envelops the identities of the starving and stifles efforts to deliver relief. Information is useless unless it circulates—it congeals in bureaucratic jargon. In the course of its

---

[18] François Jean, "Famine et Liberté de la Presse" [Famine and Freedom of the Press], *Séminaire International de L'information* [International News Weekly] (Reporters Sans Frontières, October 1989).

own famine, China revealed the devastation propaganda could produce; it took three years—and 30 million dead—for the fog of language to finally clear. The crisis never would have attained such magnitude if leaders had not been so deeply ensnared in their own illusions. Nor would the famine ever have attained such intensity if realistic data had existed to counter the official rhetoric.

Information circulates more freely in North Korea than it did in the China of the Great Leap Forward, however. Though the regime stubbornly endeavors to conceal the seriousness of the situation, some problems have at length been acknowledged and international aid actively solicited, with clear success. Since 1995, Pyongyang has been the recipient of ever increasing quantities of food aid—more than $1 billion worth over four years—and the latest appeal from the United Nations for a sum of $376 million represents the second-largest international program of relief aid—after Yugoslavia—launched in 1999. At present, food aid and concessionary trade terms appear sufficient to bridge the food shortage. Trade with China[19] and South Korea essentially serves as a supplement to international assistance. But the history of modern famines shows that famine can come about under stable conditions—even where there is a food surplus, as was the case in Bengal in 1943 and even in certain provinces of China during the Great Leap Forward. In other words, the defining feature of famine is not necessarily a shortage of food—though that may be one explanation—rather, it is the fact that some categories of the population have no access to food.[20] The central issue in a famine situation, then, is how resources are distributed to the neediest groups.

Governing authorities in democratic countries pin their credibility on their ability to implement redistributive policies and assist population groups threatened by crisis on a large scale. When information circulates

---

[19] According to unconfirmed data, China committed to sending 500,000 tons of grain, 1.3 million tons [sic] of gasoline and 2.5 million tons of coal annually until the year 2000. Heather Smith, "The Food Economy: The Catalyst for Collapse?" in *Economic Integration of the Korean Peninsula* ed. Marcus Noland (Institute for International Economics 1998). See also Scott Snyder, "North Korea's Decline and China's Strategic Dilemmas," *Special Report* (United States Institute of Peace, 1997).

[20] Amartya Sen, *Poverty and Famines* (Oxford University Press, 1981).

freely- moreover, when it is a basic component of a pluralist political system—not only does government have data on which it can act, but this very data can force it to act, via pressure from the media, opposition parties, and public response. As Amartya Sen points out, "It is hard to cite an instance of famine occurring in a country with a free press and an active opposition as part of a democratic system."[21] Nothing of the sort exists in North Korea, whose leaders seem unready to sacrifice the regime's priorities to protect one portion of the population. The problem in North Korea today is not so much the availability of resources as it is one of distribution. With international aid, it appears North Korea now possesses the means to avert famine. If it does not do so, it is out of a conscious political choice to abandon a portion of the population to its fate, rather than have it exposed to foreign view and contact.

Scarcity and Rationing

When international aid arrives in North Korea it is turned over to authorities there and then channeled through the Public Distribution System (PDS). The lack of any real opportunity over the past four years to evaluate the situation and monitor distribution has fueled questions and debate over North Korea's use of aid. The PDS's effectiveness is not at issue. For 40 years it has supervised the flow of food and supplies to the country's entire population. Neither is the diversion of aid, so often noted in the army's case, the problem. Food continues to be distributed—as it always has been—according to the regime's priorities. What is really at issue is the assumption that the regime places priority on feeding "vulnerable" population groups. Like questions about the scale of the famine, debates over the regime's use of aid demonstrate a profound misunderstanding of how the North Korean system operates.

Rationing is both a standard operating procedure and a means of social control in North Korea. In this closely supervised, perpetually mobilized society, the state provides for all of society's needs. Wages and taxes play

---

[21] Amartya Sen, "La Liberté Individuelle: Une Responsabilité Sociale" [Individual Freedoms: A Social Responsibility], *Esprit* (March 1991). See also Amartya Sen, "Pas de Bonne Èconomie Sans Vraie Démocratie" [No Sound Economy Without Real Democracy], *Le Monde* (October 1998).

only a marginal role—the population is wholly dependent on a planned, centralized system of resource allocation. Each individual is dependent on his or her work unit for access to housing, clothing, education, health care, cultural life, etc. Similarly, the entire population (except for peasant members of cooperatives) is dependent on the state for the distribution of grain, according to a complex scale that factors in social status, job, age, etc.

North Korean society is probably one of the most hierarchical in the world. As a police state, it is certainly one of the most formidable as well; its citizens are the objects of constant surveillance. Continually updated individual files determine each person's social status and position. Indeed, nowhere in the world are inequalities so deeply hardwired within an individual's "pedigree" as in North Korea. From birth individuals are classified according to their family history or their parents' status. Honor goes to children whose grandfathers died fighting for their country; they will attend the finest schools and become "pillars of the revolution." Woe to anyone whose grandfather was on the other side in the Korean War. Even his or her child will be stigmatized. Persons with cousins living in South Korea will always be under suspicion. Society is thus organized in concentric circles around the Great Leader's family, with the families of counterrevolutionaries consigned to purgatory. At the Fifth Workers' Party Conference in 1970, Kim Il Sung introduced a system of classification that organized society into three classes—a core class, a suspect "wavering" class, and a hostile class—and 51 categories.[22] Since that time the system has been modified during periodic phases of reclassification, but every individual's status is still determined by political loyalty and family history. This complex hierarchy governs every aspect of social life. Obviously it determines opportunities to rise to senior positions in the party and the army—but it also affects access to material goods. Class membership leads not only to privileged access to education and promotions to positions of responsibility but also to the perks and privileges these entail: cars, special stores, heated apartments, health care, etc.

Food distribution involves enormous disparities, as well, and is closely

---

[22] Asia Watch, Human Rights in the Democratic People's Republic of Korea (1988).

regulated. Other criteria enter in besides class, such as age or type of work. These determine grain (or, in the past, fish or meat) allowances to the very gram. In the 1970s daily ration levels ranged from 800 grams of rice—for workers in heavy industry, military aviation, or senior party officials—to 200 grams of a mix of poor-quality grains for those trapped in groups classified as hostile and condemned to waste away. Here again, circumstances changed after a series of "patriotic withholdings" were deducted from rations in the 1970s and 1980s and when drastic cuts were later ordered under the "hard march" of recent years. With no grain to distribute, the PDS's role began to diminish in the early 1990s. Later, rations were reduced even in Pyongyang and the army. Then, in the mid-1990s, the PDS ceased to function completely in certain regions and for certain population categories.[23] Some groups were dropped from the system, particularly those who were "tainted" socially, or worked for idle factories, or lived in remote regions—more often than not these things coincide. In the climate of acute scarcity that emerged during the 1990s, this non-egalitarian system of resource allocation had tragic consequences for some population categories.

Famine and the System

As circumstances worsened in the mid-1990s, the rationing system hit bottom. Faced with shortages of such magnitude, the regime tacitly abandoned all efforts to feed the entire population. With the centralized system of resource allocation unable to carry out its functions, its responsibilities devolved to the provincial and local levels. This de facto decentralization had a particularly sharp impact on certain regions, which appear to have been cut off from distribution channels and left to their fate. The accounts of refugees who managed to reach China reveal that, for example, distribution of supplies was suspended from 1994 onwards in the provinces of Hamgyong, Yanggang, and Chagan. Because most of the refugees were natives of these border areas we have little data on other regions, but it would be no great surprise if these remote, sparsely inhab-

---

[23] Sue Lautze, *The Famine in North Korea: Humanitarian Responses in Communist Nations* (Feinstein International Famine Center, Tufts University, June 1997).

ited provinces were among the hardest hit. There are several reasons for this: inadequate transportation and lack of fuel supply for these provinces, which are distant from the capital and the agricultural regions of the country's southwest; or too few influential apparatchiks to secure distribution; or too many persons of no importance in these traditional regions of exile. Most important: the absence of any economic advantage—due to idle factories and closed mines, subsistence agriculture—in these mountainous regions in the northern latitudes ...

Nevertheless, the famine is not circumscribed geographically. First, because in a country where individuals are assigned to work units, where all displacement is monitored, and where only the privileged are authorized to live in Pyongyang, geographic location often merely mirrors and coincides with political classification. Second, and most important, because even in neglected regions, favored categories of citizens have continued to receive a certain minimal amount of food. The food shortage may have virtually drained the distribution system dry, but it has not caused it to disappear entirely. The regime adapted itself to scarcity without allowing its priorities to be undermined—if anything, they were reaffirmed. Rather than undermine the dogma of food self-reliance by importing food or trying to establish a safety net for the most vulnerable, the regime concentrated its meager resources on groups that were the most instrumental to the system's survival and the functioning of the economy. Paradoxically, the flow of international aid through these official channels revitalized them to some degree, and may have reinforced this discriminatory approach. Perhaps there was no other choice in a country where every aspect of social life is controlled by the regime. In North Korea, famine is deeply woven into the fabric of privilege the regime has constructed. It is a social, not a geographic, fact.

Traditionally favored groups have continued to receive their rations, however reduced, throughout the 1990s. This has obviously been true for army and party cadres, who also have access to special stores, can obtain special currency, and, above all, possess a key resource in such circumstances—political leverage—which allows them not only to get by, but to profit from the situation. Similarly, those employed in strategically valuable factories—either military related or likely to generate foreign currency—are considered a workforce to be sustained at any cost. Finally, the army still receives top priority—all the more so due to its steadily enhanced role since Kim Il Sung's death. Members of agricultural cooperatives are the only population category not dependent on state grain allowances. Beyond the portion allotted them at harvest time, they have since the 1980s been allowed any surpluses over and above quota amounts belonging to the state—at least in theory. Everything, of course, depends on how production goals are set, given the tendency to one-upmanship. Nevertheless, except when harvests are poor, peasants are rather less badly off than laborers or employees, if only because they can cultivate their own patches of land or illegal plots in the hills. Generally speaking, the most vulnerable population groups appear to be inhabitants of rural areas not employed in agriculture or city dwellers dependent on state-distributed rations and not employed in strategic sectors. Pyongyang residents are still spared; though living in buildings without heating or fuel is hardly comfortable, the capital remains the regime's showcase, where members of hostile classes are not authorized to live. But in the stricken smaller cities, a world of dilapidated buildings and idle factories, those people not considered politically loyal or economically useful no longer receive food and are left to their fate.

Starving

This population, which was dependent on the state for three generations and is now left to fend for itself, has had to improvise in order to survive; in just a few years bartering and trading have become widespread. Peasant markets, previously authorized to operate three times a month, are now held daily in cities and at roadsides, selling grains at prohibitive prices, plants and shellfish gathered here and there, furniture, and anything else people are driven by poverty to sell. Products from China are also sold— medicines or clothing brought over the border. This small-scale trade, just barely tolerated by the authorities, has become the main alternative for the people who have been cut off. But in the end, many cannot get by on these transactions—a kind of shabby echo of the caloric trade-offs the regime practices in its foreign trade—which just barely provide them a bit of cornstarch for their soup. Some die in silence from hunger, illness, and exhaustion. Others, often survivors of shattered families, turn to migration as a last resort. In a society where leaving one's family and work unit means losing every kind of support and social standing, very few take to the road. In a country where neither work nor ration allowances are available outside of the official system, no one knows where to go. In a system where every displacement is closely monitored, this mobility seems nevertheless to be tolerated. Perhaps it is because these migrants and, often, these abandoned children, have become phantoms. The regime simply averts its gaze; these displaced persons, beyond reach of international aid, have vanished from society—they do not exist in the North Korean system. Some make it to China, where they stay a few days or a few months. They try to find food, medicine, assistance, or work, then usually return to help their families. These refugees or migrants who have been able to reach China are the only North Koreans with whom it is possible to speak freely.[24] They are doubtless not typical of the country's population as a whole: first, because they often come from the border regions and second, because they have left their families and work units, a step very few can bring themselves to take. But they do accurately reflect the fate of persons cut off from support, the vulnerable populations humanitarian organizations speak of and for whom international aid is, in theory, intended. There are perhaps—no one knows—five to six million people cut off from support in North Korea, a quarter of the country's population. In recent years they have died by the hundreds of thousands. If nothing changes, they will continue to die by the hundreds of thousands in the years to come.

---

[24] Interviews conducted by Médecins Sans Frontières with refugees at the Chinese border in April and August 1998. See "Corée du Nord, Récits d'une Famine Cachée" [North Korea, Accounts of a Hidden Famine], *Libération* (September 1998); see also surveys conducted by the Korean Buddhist Sharing Movement among North Korean refugees in China, 1997–98.

Section Two
Conflict

CHAPTER FOUR

Security: How Do We Know When Not To Go Too Far?

Originally published in *Messages*, No. 42, Oct.1991

Again and again Somalia and Liberia bring us back to the issue of security. Not that we had ever set it aside, but because in these instances it is still so unresolved. There is no façade of legality to appeal to, no army to be bound by the Geneva Conventions, nothing to constrain those carrying Kalashnikovs. There are no politics, ultimately, behind these unsolvable conflicts—too much clan mentality, too much gang rage. There are no politics—at least none that can be readily comprehended and deciphered in binary terms that would apply elsewhere on the planet. As superficial as it might have been, the ideological threat of the Cold War was in a sense reassuring. It gave structure to a system we claimed we were transcending in order to focus solely on the victims, and we could assume our counterparts in the dialogue cared about their international image and credibility. Not that we mourn the Cold War or feel nostalgic for a system peopled by obscure despots, liberator-guerillas, and captive populations. Good riddance, Siad Barre and Samuel Doe!

Nevertheless, Somalia and Liberia are troubling examples of forgotten wars, from Mozambique to Afghanistan—privatized, criminalized conflicts, continually recurring and breaking down at every level along clan, ethnic, or religious lines. The values we claim to represent are barely audible above the din of these clashing identity groups. To be sure, there has never really been such a thing as immunity for humanitarian workers. But the risk now is of our being perceived by the bearers of Kalashnikovs as no more than foreigners with an odd way of conducting themselves. Naturally, we mean to change that perception, convinced as we are that "the South" is not some no-man's-land where our teams can land and fan out to provide medical treatment for bodies, just as parachutists are deployed by others to extract their nationals from a situation of pervasive barbarity. Liberia and Somalia are not peopled with cardboard figures. They are men and women we can help, with whom we want to work and interact, even if we are the only ones left, in the end, who refuse to give up all for lost.

If we are to remain, we must not, in any event, lose sight of the hazards of war anyone would normally try to guard against. In these crisis situations it is essential to protect oneself and to prepare for any eventuality. It is all the more important to realize that we are outsiders—moreover that we carry dollars—and that our perspective on events takes us precisely where populations are the most threatened, the injured most numerous, and the combatants the most nervous. The wish to reach civilians trapped by fighting should be weighed against the concern to protect ourselves so we may continue to act. It is up to us to be clearheaded enough to limit our risks and know exactly when not to go too far.

But security is not confined to prudent measures and evacuation procedures alone. It is the result of day-to-day conduct, of understanding a society, of being able to size up situations—situations that are fluid, volatile, and uncertain, their twists and turns difficult to grasp. Seemingly inextricable crisis situations, where it is necessary to grasp the dynamics without getting bogged down in the complexity ... Knowledge of the context does not mean much, in the end, if we cannot move ahead with greater assuredness and effectiveness. It is useless to understand, if in doing so we are to lose all objectivity, all perception of what is at stake, or any sense of what our position is. Either from habit or familiarity, one could forget that we are not present merely by chance. We are there to help people trapped by war, without discriminating in any way.

In these conflicts that concern us in their human dimensions alone, the worst that could happen is that we be perceived as an interested party. Neutrality is not only an essential principal in and of itself; it is a significant factor for our security. So it should be clearly displayed—in the spirit of Médecins Sans Frontières's charter and the Geneva Conventions, of course, but most important on a day-to-day basis, in the impartiality of our actions, the evenhandedness of our interventions, and the independence of our decisions. We cannot be sure, in any event, that this position of neutrality will really be taken into account by warring parties. Nor can we be sure it will be understood in Somalia and Liberia. In nebulous situations such as these, where the number of protagonists continues to increase and war is fueled by plunder, one must know how to distance oneself from all of the parties to the conflict. One must also know how to earn respect on the basis of impartial actions and predictable conduct. In short, one must be able to guard against every form of excess, aided by that instinct we call common sense.

CHAPTER FIVE

Have You Heard About Somalia?

Originally pubished in *Croissance*, March 1992

On January 27, 1991, Siad Barre fled Mogadishu in defeat after violent fighting that was virtually buried in the news headlines by the furor surrounding the Gulf War. One year later, celebrating that anniversary would occur to absolutely no one. In reality the fighting did not stop, and recent developments inspire little optimism. The bloody dictatorship of Siad Barre has given way to a power struggle that is pushing the country into a spiral of violence and destruction. No one knows exactly what remains of Somalia itself, any longer—between the North, which has declared its independence, and the numerous territories formed and reshaped in every corner of the country whenever fighting flares up again. Any semblance of rule of law has thoroughly vanished in the capital, which is now a battleground for clans wrangling over the spoils of a state that has long since collapsed.

The fighting that began in mid-November between the followers of President Ali Mahdi Mohammed and those of General Mohammed Farrah Aidid has succeeded in reducing Mogadishu to a stretch of ruins, abandoned to looting and random gunfire. And—anywhere at any hour—pickup trucks, the poor man's armored car, shuttle to and fro spinning the web of this endless fighting. Mogadishu is empty, abandoned by its residents, who have sought refuge in the outskirts of the capital. The nomads, with their weapons and clan mentality, hold the city now. Still, to every cloud its silver lining: this clan mentality, not at all helpful for reaching a political solution, has its own rules and boundaries nonetheless. Or at least let us hope so—because as the conflict further degenerates, it is sometimes hard to tell the difference between warring clans and gangs on the rampage.

The consequences for the population in this forgotten conflict are tragic. Uprooted groups crisscross the entire country, shifting about to avoid the fighting or seeking refuge in neighboring countries in an effort to find some means of subsistence and a measure of safety. Displaced persons and refugees number in the hundreds of thousands, and there are tens of thousands of wounded. In the city of Mogadishu alone, Médecins Sans Frontières (MSF) estimates the number of wounded treated at clinics since mid-November at 20,000, and the number of deaths at more than 8,000. Graves line the roadways. Hospitals are swamped—when they are not being shelled—and no one can say what will become of the displaced persons in the areas surrounding the capital and all across the country.

In the absence of any international presence—aside from Egyptian and Sudanese diplomatic representatives—only a handful of humanitarian organizations remain as witnesses to the Somali ordeal. Their principal dilemma in Mogadishu, like elsewhere, is gaining access to civilians trapped by the fighting. More than elsewhere, however, their freedom of action in Mogadishu is sharply limited by the intransigence of the warring parties. In the absence of any neutral force, the atmosphere of danger is such that humanitarian organizations are being forced to rely on the clans themselves for protection. As indispensable as it is, this protection can quickly become a straitjacket. From our "protectors'" perspective there is only the haziest distinction between concern for our security and the desire to monopolize our aid—to shield us from any unpleasant encounters with representatives of other clans.

Aid is an all-important prize for warring parties in Somalia; it is also a vital resource for population groups under threat—particularly food aid, which is difficult to relay. Because of this it is essential to remain accessible to everyone, to assess needs with complete independence, and to respond to those needs without discrimination of any kind. So we need to go back and forth between the front lines on a regular basis, resupply medical structures regardless of which side of the lines they are on, work to keep hospitals neutral, see to it that they are weapon-free, guarantee unimpeded access to medical care for the wounded of all the warring parties, gain access to displaced persons on the periphery of the country, and attempt to get food to the neediest.

For a year now, MSF has been trying to maintain and carve out more space for humanitarian action. Without it, these groups would be hopelessly stranded amid war and famine. But our efforts will be in vain if they are not taken up, in turn, by the international community. Somalia is at the edge of the abyss. Every attempt must be made to reinitiate a dialogue and foster a climate that allows humanitarian aid to be distributed effectively to those population groups most urgently in need.

CHAPTER SIX

The Sudanese Conflict

Originally published in the quarterly *Catholica*, February 1993, www.catholica.fr

Catholica: *For brief periods, Somalia and Bosnia made the ratings jump. Not so with Sudan. Is there nothing special at all going on there?*

François Jean: Since 1983 the country has been devastated, once again, by war. Sudan has actually been through a series of wars, each rooted in the deep ethnic, religious, and historical cleavage between the Arab-Muslim north and the black-African south, which is mainly Christian and animist. The south has always been in a sense disadvantaged economically—not to mention being robbed, in a sense, by people in the north with no desire to share the nation's resources.

The first war broke out even before the country's independence in 1955 and lasted until 1972, the year the Addis Ababa accords were signed. Then there was a period of respite, but this was relatively brief. Fighting set in again as early as 1983; just recently it has reached such a level of intensity that it is now reasonable to speculate if it is not tantamount to genocide. The number of victims is estimated at about 10 percent of the south's population—or roughly six hundred thousand people out of six million. There have been three overall phases in this exceptionally bitter war. In the first, the conflict was "normal," although it did bring about major population displacements. The second, so-called "democratic," phase coincided with the coming to power of Sadek al-Mahdi. The new regime formulated a strategy based on exploiting ethnic antagonisms, and their first step was to arm tribal militias. There has always been friction between the shepherds of the north and those of the south, taking the form of raids and cattle theft. The regime deliberately stoked these antagonisms, arming a group of Islamized nomads known as the Baggara to do battle with those in the south who allegedly—and this is not entirely untrue—provide the base of support for the Sudanese People's Liberation Army (SPLA) created in 1983 by John Garang, then an officer in the

Sudanese Army. This was a period of large-scale massacres, of which little was really known because they occurred in a remote, hard to reach region. Also, it must be added, there was a very serious famine following the 1988 drought that, unlike the famine in Ethiopia, has never been discussed.

A new phase began in 1989 when, to everyone's surprise, the National Islamic Front came to power. The Egyptians, in any case, greeted the change with clear satisfaction, believing the new regime would be ready to negotiate an end to the conflict. But the reality was entirely different—it turned out to be no more than an Islamist takeover of power led by Hassan al-Turabi. Instead of being abandoned, the previous regime's use of tribal militias instead became more widespread. At this time, a policy of mass deportation was implemented, as well, with the aim of transforming the nation's ethnic and religious balance. Over a million and a half people fleeing war in the south gravitated to the outskirts of Khartoum, seeking a measure of security and some means of subsistence. Under the pretext of urban planning and environmental conservation, the government targeted shantytowns, clearing them with bulldozers. The now-homeless inhabitants were forcibly transferred to the desert and left to the mercies of Islamist organizations, the only groups authorized to work in the new camps. They say that one of the masterminds of this policy was recently honored at the Rio Environmental Summit. (Something similar happened during the massive 1998 famine—the world's attention was captivated far more by three whales trapped in ice than by hundreds of thousands of people dying in southern Sudan.) Moreover there were also massive displacements from the north to the south, as well, particularly in southern Kordofan. Because it is so difficult to gain access to Sudan, it is not always easy to confirm information, but it seems quite certain that these displacements, far from being solely attributable to the war, are part of an overall plan.

And what are the main features of the current regime?

FJ: This regime means to re-instruct everyone in the principles of Islam. Sudan was once organized around the major Islamic religious orders. The regime wants to get rid of every form of popular religion and go back to the letter of the law of Islam—as revised and corrected by their own Islamic ideology. Yet, insofar as the regime is addressing the nation's economic and technological development, it may, from the outside, appear to be a modern or modernizing country. As a result, Sudanese specialists find themselves in a highly equivocal position vis-à-vis the regime. As experts, they do not want to lose their access to the field and are prepared to keep silent if it means they can continue their research. The regime also holds a certain fascination for them, particularly from the viewpoint of its rhetoric regarding economic efficiency: the explanation that the trains run on time is used to justify the ruling order—the old argument used by admirers of Mussolini in his day ... For my part, I can't help but reply, "Yes, they certainly do run on time—packed with deportees." So there is a very heavy ideological presence, and the repression affects everyone, even Muslims. In Darfur, western Sudan, an uprising recently occurred that reinforced government fears of spreading unrest among the black-African population, especially Islamized-black Africans. The repression is appalling. The government is terribly afraid of the SPLA's influence taking root among these Muslim populations. Additionally, there is a deliberate intent on the part of the Khartoum government to impede any aid from reaching threatened populations. So United Nations officials are constantly being given the runaround: they are forever waiting for travel or flight authorizations. The administrative and bureaucratic obstacles thoroughly undermine any attempt to assist people.

Having said all this, how would you explain the widespread lack of interest in the Sudanese issue?

FJ: One of the reasons, surely, is the impenetrability of the Khartoum regime. We're dealing with a truly oppressive atmosphere. No one knows what is going on, because no one has access to the most endangered populations. All we know is that there are massive population displacements and forced deportations, and that hundreds of thousands of people are threatened by famine. Media coverage is important to build public awareness, but in Sudan's case there really seems to be no interest and, far more, a deliberate intent to conceal the seriousness of the situation.

Interview by Stéphen de Petiville

CHAPTER SEVEN

What Role for MSF?

Originally published in *Messages*, No. 60, May 1993

Somalia, Iraq, Bosnia, Angola … so begins the long list of situations that raise fundamental questions about our capacity for action in environments undergoing radical change. It is certainly not the first time we have been confronted with genuine difficulties. During our more than 20 years of interventions in every kind of crisis zone, we have had to overcome serious security problems, the indifference of the international community, and the intransigence of warring parties in order to bring medical relief to population groups at risk. Our only passport has been our independence and impartiality, and our only safety net, when political actors attempt to mobilize humanitarian aid, has been to keep a clear head.

But we have never been in the line of fire to such a degree as we are now or so often had to question what our role should be. It happened in Somalia: recruiting guards, at the risk of adding fuel to the war economy; then, faced with famine, appealing to the international community even if it meant dealing with a military intervention and, in the end, being smothered by excessive protection in a climate of total confusion. Along with Yugoslavia, Somalia is probably one of the most remarkable examples of the difficulty of delivering humanitarian aid in an environment of fragmenting conflicts and an increasing number of intervening parties.

Since the Cold War, crises have both increased in number and changed in character. Political or ideological opposition movements have given way to religious, nationalist, and ethnic antagonisms. Guerilla movements, deprived of superpower support, have splintered into myriad armed groups and are operating as pure predators. The values we claim to represent are barely audible above the din of these clashing identities. Humanitarian organizations are more than ever seen as targets, and access to victims is more and more problematic. What is to be done? Can we be satisfied with distributing medicines if it means we can no longer guarantee our con-

tinuous presence on the ground? Must we resort to armed protection, if
it means sacrificing our principles for the sake of short-term pragmatism?
Should we appeal for international intervention if that means further blurring the line between military and humanitarian action? Certainly governments are now more inclined than ever to act on humanitarian terrain. In
an odd reversal, wars have become ever more privatized and criminalized,
while the humanitarian sphere is increasingly militarized and government
centered ... The growing involvement of governments raises the question
of how we should position ourselves vis-à-vis other actors in an increasingly crowded humanitarian field. How do we interact and, if necessary,
collaborate with governments and the United Nations without losing our
independence and freedom of action? How do we avoid the absorption, the
domination, even, of the humanitarian by the political? What do we expect
of governments and the international community?

The days are gone when, faced with a tragic situation, we could be satisfied with calling for an international response. We are entering a more
complex environment, and we must now make our expectations more
explicit. We also need to rethink our overall strategic goals, our capacity
for action, our methods of intervention, and where and when we take
a stand. MSF's upcoming general assembly on May 15–16 gives us the
opportunity to have this important debate on the role of Médecins Sans
Frontières in these new crisis zones.

Chapter Eight

Necessary Independence

Originally published in the journal *La Provence,* December 20, 1997

Murders in Burundi, Chechnya, Rwanda ... kidnappings in Chechnya and Tajikistan. For several months such tragedies have been relentlessly on the rise; now humanitarian aid workers often pay dearly indeed for their efforts to deliver assistance to endangered populations.

There has been a very real deterioration of security conditions for international organizations intervening in crisis situations. Yet this is not due to any radical change in the nature of conflicts themselves. Contrary to a widely held notion, the end of the Cold War has not brought us a period of disorder, anarchy, or chaos and violence that is bloodier, more senseless, or more irrational than ever before. Disillusioning though this may be for those who are nostalgic for a lost golden age, immunity for humanitarian workers has never existed, and relief organizations intervening in civil wars or internal conflicts have always faced a multitude of obstacles—as well as threats—in their efforts to deliver aid to victims of conflict or repression.

Still, these troubles have increased in number in recent years, especially during that most perilous phase immediately following a cease-fire (which, in theory, should usher in a period of peace ...)—a time when some armed groups begin to break down into detached, privatized, criminal gangs, reorganized on the basis of looting and racketeering. But the principal difference relates back to the aid system's remarkable evolution over the last decade. At the close of the 1980s, the preponderance of international aid for crisis situations was distributed on the peripheries of conflicts in refugee camps, with only a few rare humanitarian organizations intervening directly to aid people trapped by the fighting.

Since then the number of relief operations in conflict zones has rapidly increased; there is now a profusion of UN programs and nongovernmental initiatives, Blue Helmets and multinational forces. At the same time, emergency aid budgets have grown sixfold, encouraging the blossoming of organizations without experience in crisis situations.

A consequence of this rapid growth in the number of organizations of all sorts now present in arenas of conflict—private, state based, or even military—is that local populations and armed groups now have a more muddled perception of humanitarian actors. In some countries such as Somalia or Bosnia, humanitarian organizations are confused with the military. Elsewhere they are believed to be associated with their governments. In every case they are perceived as rich and Western ...

Under such conditions, it is more important than ever for humanitarian organizations to keep their distance from the military, to overtly demonstrate their independence with respect to political authorities, to leave behind the established international circles in the capital cities in order to get closer to the people—in short, to reaffirm the core principles of humanitarian action: impartiality, independence, and solidarity. It is also fundamentally important in crises such as these that are not "humanitarian" but highly political, with all their violence and repression, to show clearheadedness, caution, and determination in order to preserve ourselves and protect the victims.

CHAPTER NINE

Mission Impossible ...
on The Back Roads Of Chechnya

Originally published in *Messages*, No. 87, September-October 1996

Grozny, Chechnya: François Jean of Médecins Sans Frontières (MSF) *Fondation* and Vincent de Bellefroid, MSF head of mission, attempted to aid hundreds of civilians trapped in the besieged capital. Supported by the inhabitants—and in spite of obstacles raised by the Russian military—they were able to provide medical relief to health care facilities still in operation ...

How did Grozny fall at the beginning of August?

Fighters infiltrated Grozny during the night of August 6 and captured most of the capital within two days. But there was still some very hard fighting for more than a week around the pro-Russian government buildings and entrenched camps where federal forces had fallen back. The response of the Russian troops was, unfortunately, typical of their practices since the beginning of the conflict: massive artillery shelling and aerial bombing, random firing, sniper harassment, etc. These blind reprisals caused significant casualties—hundreds of civilians were killed or wounded and the residents of the worst-affected neighborhoods hid in their cellars for days on end without water or electricity and no way of evacuating the injured.

What kind of medical treatment did the injured have access to during the fighting?

Opportunities for providing treatment were once again quite limited for three basic reasons: first, the difficulty of transporting the injured in a city fragmented by fighting and leveled by bombing; second, the condition of the hospitals; five days after the start of the fighting, most of the surgical units—except for Hospitals Three and Five and one temporary structure set up in a school—had either been evacuated or destroyed; third—and this goes back to the same problem—the lack of security in the health facilities. During the tensest periods, most of the injured weren't staying in the hospitals. They were transported there—whenever possible—and operated on, but then sent right back home or evacuated to peripheral units. For example, when we went to Polyclinic 6 for the first time, six seriously injured persons, two of them little girls about 10 years old, arrived within a half an hour. But when we went back the next day there was no one left. The unit was empty.

How do you explain why people avoided the health facilities?

The hospitals weren't secure—it wasn't safe to be there—for two main reasons. First, health facilities weren't spared by the bombing. In Chechnya a hospital is a target like any other, and maybe more so ... For example, Hospital Four was attacked from the very first day of fighting even though, according to different sources, there was no fighting in that neighborhood. According to our sources, Russian helicopters targeted the hospital deliberately (one of the rockets made a direct hit on the operating theatre, killing three nurses, three doctors, and the person on the operating table); it was partially destroyed and then evacuated. The second reason why patients, and particularly the men, wouldn't stay in the hospitals was that they were not provided with protection. On the fifth day of fighting a Russian unit went into Hospital Nine looking for injured people likely to become combatants. The troops' arrival provoked clashes with combatants present in the neighborhood, and the hospital had to be evacuated under very difficult circumstances—nurses were killed, some of the injured were scattered among neighboring houses. Others, along with some of the staff, took shelter in the International Committee of the Red Cross (ICRC) delegation ...

What activities were you able to keep up during the combat phase?

When we got caught up in the war we were in the midst of relaunching MSF activities in Chechnya … We ended up trapped by the fighting without much in the way of resources, but we decided not to stay on the sidelines. We managed to get out of the city on foot and reach a neighboring republic, Ingushetia, where we had our medical stocks. We shuttled back and forth that way between Nazran and Grozny for 15 days, getting medical and surgical aid into the Chechen capital and getting emergency supplies to the rare health facilities that were still operating.

What was the attitude of the Russian military?

We were dealing with a deliberate intent to block any aid from getting into the capital. We were facing the same obstacles we had faced last March and April in the cities of Sernovodsk and Samashki, where humanitarian aid was prohibited for many, many weeks after the bombings and the "cleaning up" operations … We were blocked at Russian checkpoints set up on the principal access routes to Grozny, so we had to take back roads and cut across fields, or go on foot, blending in with the population. We were interacting closely with people all during that time, working our contacts and looking for allies on the same side—and we found them.

A lot of people helped us, they could see we were sticking our own necks out—that we were involved and determined. Even if our mission was limited (but could we have done any more with full charters?), it was an amazing collective experience; we gave hundreds of injured the chance to be treated.

What were your operational goals after Russia and Chechnya signed their peace accord?

After the August 22 cease-fire the situation became more and more stable. We left Grozny and picked up where we left off with our projects. We got our project in Chatoi going. Of course, relaunching our mission in Chechnya means we have to be ready to respond to any emergency situation that might again arise in this devastated country.

CHAPTER TEN

The Problems Of Medical Relief In Chechen War Zones

Originally published in English in *Central Asian Survey*, 15 (2), 1996

Médecins Sans Frontières has been working in the North Caucasus for almost two years. We first intervened in Ingushetia to bring assistance to Ingush refugees from the Prigorodny district in North Ossetia.

In the summer of 1994 we extended our activities to Chechnya from our base in Nazran. Our program focused on helping the medical authorities in their efforts to cope with the cholera epidemic in the eastern part of the republic. We also delivered medical supplies to hospitals where there was an acute shortage of drugs, due partly to the embargo imposed on Chechnya by the Russian authorities.

From September 1994, the increasing tension and medical shortages in Chechnya led us to progressively increase our intervention in response to the ever growing needs.

In early December the "open phase of the crisis" began, and the war broke out. Confronted with the dramatic and ever growing human consequences of the conflict, we considerably expanded our presence and assistance.

From December 1994 until the end of February 1995, we concentrated on assisting the overcrowded hospitals around Grozny and south of the capital. We also reinforced our team in Nazran and began activities in Khasavyurt to bring assistance to the huge numbers of refugees pouring into Ingushetia and Dagestan.

From early March, while continuing our assistance to refugees and displaced people, we tried to help reestablish a minimal degree of medical service in Grozny. This involved the reopening and resupplying of the hospitals and polyclinics devastated by fighting and heavy shelling.

During this same period, we installed permanent medical and surgical missions in the southern part of the country. This permanent presence in the regions which were not yet under the control of the Russian forces was all the more important for the fact that the civilian population was most at risk in these areas threatened by military offensives and bombardments or air raids. Over these three months, we did our best to bring assistance to people in need (particularly displaced persons) and to treat the increasing number of wounded in this region, which was most affected by fighting and shelling.

In mid-February, we installed a medical mission in Kurtchaloi and, at the end of March, another team settled in Chatoi, where it worked until an ultimatum from the Russian military authorities forced it to evacuate on June 2, 1995, along with wounded people under treatment. In the meantime, another surgical team was installed in Vedeno at the beginning of February. In early April, the increasing number of fighters present in the town convinced the team to hand over to a Chechen medical team and to move to Marketi, where it reestablished medical and surgical services for the civilian population.

*****

Despite all our efforts, it must be said that we largely failed to answer all the needs. The reasons for our shortcomings were numerous:

- the extent of the needs,
- the few NGOs present in Chechnya,
- the total absence of UN agencies,
- the lack of diplomatic support by the so called "international community,"
- the obstacles set by the Russian military authorities hindering relief assistance in Chechnya, particularly in war zones,
- and, last but not least, the sheer brutality of this war mainly aimed at civilians, with little respect for relief convoys or medical installations.

I will now discuss the last two points in more detail. First, the problem of gaining access to the victims was very acute in the case of Chechnya. From the end of February, no authorization was given for relief convoys to enter conflict zones. Furthermore, cars were frequently stopped at checkpoints.

Despite these repeated obstacles, we managed to overcome part of the problem by multiplying our supply trips using cars loaded with medicines.

In a context of frequent gunfire on roads, this strategy, undertaken at great personal risk by our teams, allowed us to maintain a minimal stock in our hospitals in the south. Although it was an imperfect answer for the problem of medical supply, it was not a solution for general relief—food, shelter, etc.—which was most needed in March and early April, at a time when the southern part of the country was being flooded with displaced people fleeing the heavy bombing in Grozny, Argun, Gudermes and Shali …

At the end of April, the situation improved, partly because many of the displaced people moved northward to try to reestablish themselves in their places of origin or to seek refuge in Ingushetia and Dagestan, and partly because the military authorities were more accommodating in light of the May 9 celebrations in Moscow. But only days after the end of the celebrations, we faced renewed and increasing pressure and obstacles from military authorities.

These obstacles were twofold. First, there were continuous administrative difficulties. Throughout our intervention, we had been suspected of contravening a multiplicity of rules and regulations, sometimes contradictory, on issues such as customs, visas, registration. Such difficulties reflect both the complexity of Russian red tape and the political reticence to allow independent NGOs to intervene in Chechnya. In any event, it greatly reduced our ability to react rapidly and with flexibility to the needs of the population.

Second, there were deliberate attempts by the Russian forces to forbid any kind of assistance for the regions of Chechnya that were not under their control. We had, on many occasions, the strong impression that some military authorities were not willing to make a distinction between civilians and fighters. I myself remember a conversation with a high-ranking general—a true dialogue of the deaf—when our focus on assistance to the civilian population was systematically met with accusations of helping the fighters.

Not withstanding the difficulties encountered by humanitarian organizations, I must highlight the dramatic human consequences of the war.

After the bloody failure of their first attempts to enter Grozny, Russian military authorities adopted a brutal strategy at considerable cost to the civilian population. For several weeks Grozny was subjected to heavy artillery and aviation bombing until Russian forces were able to occupy the ruins.

The gravity of this strategy should not be underestimated. There have been a great number of comparisons in the media between Chechnya and Afghanistan or between Grozny and Beirut or Sarajevo. But if I were to give my personal opinion on the issue, I would say that the tragedy of Grozny reminds me of the fate of Hargeisa, razed to the ground by Siad Barre in 1988, or Hama, when it was submitted to heavy bombardment in February 1982 and then subjected to bloody repression by Syrian security forces. In these three situations national authorities deliberately destroyed large cities on their territory and exposed their own citizens to indiscriminate shelling. The paradox, in the case of Grozny, is that the Russian population was the main victim of the bombings at a time when most Chechen families were able to find refuge with relatives outside the capital.

Once Grozny had been reduced to rubble, other towns such as Argun, Shali and Gudermes were also partly destroyed by indiscriminate shelling without any consideration for the fate of civilians.

This kind of strategy is unacceptable. Indiscriminate and disproportionate attacks on civilian locations—including schools, hospitals—are a flagrant violation of international humanitarian law and the Geneva Conventions.

The civilian population was not only the main victim of this war, but it was also, in a way, held hostage and submitted to heavy reprisals and collective punishment. In the event of an act of resistance, the whole village risked being shelled and destroyed.

One consequence of this type of war can now be clearly seen in Chechnya in the overwhelming number of new tombs found in every village or town cemetery. Furthermore, hospitals that were overburdened during the worst periods of shelling also witnessed the direct consequences of this type of war. To take only one example, in Chatoi from May 16 to May 25, our team performed 50 surgical interventions on warwounded people under general anesthesia. Of these 50 cases, 33 were major operations and most of the wounded were civilians. I should add at this point that during the worst periods, at the end of May, we had to operate in the cellar of a private house because the hospital itself was insufficiently safe in a context of indiscriminate air bombardments.

Apart from indiscriminate shelling and disproportionate attacks on civilian locations, we heard of numerous cases of exactions, executions, looting, and abuses in the period following the fighting. We were also aware of widespread detentions in "filtration points" and prisons with clear violations of human rights, including beating, torture, and mistreatment. In general, it seems that looting and racketeering continued for a long period in many places in Chechnya.

Human rights organizations, though, are better placed to broach these subjects than we are. Our duty is to concentrate on treating the victims, and we have neither the time nor the mandate to undertake systematic inquiries on individual cases of human rights violations. Nevertheless the work of human rights organizations should be given strong support at this stage. The killing still continues under a different guise. War gives way to a cruel cycle of ambush and reprisals. It is therefore more important than ever to call for the respect of human rights.

For our part, we have been trying, since December 1994, to focus the attention of public opinion and democratic countries on the flagrant violations of international humanitarian law in the conflict.

Unfortunately, we have met with very little success. There have been some protests but these have lacked in strength. The European Union postponed, for a while, the signing of an interim agreement. But the climate of the G7 summit in Halifax, Nova Scotia, showed that the general indifference to the Chechens' fate could easily turn to concession and even connivance with Russia's leaders.

Not to denounce the utter contempt for civilian lives shown by Russian leadership is most worrying. The excuse of the Chechen crisis being an internal matter doesn't alter the problem at all. All states, and particularly democracies, have an obligation "to observe and to ensure observance" for the Geneva Conventions.

The last year was, for humanitarian organizations, a year of disillusionment. After Rwanda, where genocide was allowed to happen live on TV screens without any reaction from the so-called "international community," Chechnya now highlights the gap between knowledge and conscience and the fact that the worst may happen in a climate of total impunity.

CHAPTER ELEVEN

Chechnya: Moscow's Revenge Statistics Included

Originally published in English in *Harvard International Review*, September 22, 2000, no. 3, vol. 22

The Human Rights Debacle in Chechnya

The period of respite is over. After three years of uneasy calm, Chechnya once more finds itself in the grip of war. The Khasavyurt Accords of August 31, 1996, which brought an end to two years of conflict, were ultimately nothing more than a brief hiatus in the centuries-old confrontation between Russians and Chechens. It did not take long for the excesses generated by the anarchy in Grozny to be manipulated by the cynical maneuvers of the Kremlin oligarchy and for Chechnya to be set once more on the road to confrontation with Russia. It seemed inevitable that Chechnya, marked by two centuries of resistance to Russian colonialism and so recently devastated by fighting (December 1994 to August 1996), would once again fall into a morass of violence and conflict.

After three years, the course of history appears to be repeating itself. It would be comical if it were not so disastrous for Chechnya, Russia, and the Caucasus. This new war will be even crueler than the previous war, which decimated the Chechen population. It will be a more absurd war, too, because neither of the two goals formulated by Russia's reckless leaders—the "liquidation of terrorists" and the "liberation of Chechnya"—is likely to be achieved. And it will also be a more worrisome war because it casts a particularly harsh light on the present state of Russia's social and political systems and threatens to drag the entire Caucasus into the dispute.

State in Crisis

For the past three years, Chechnya has been in a state of limbo, tormented both by de facto independence and a state of anarchy that is liable to degenerate into fratricidal conflict. Because the Chechen state has been unable to assert its legitimacy and the Chechen leader Aslan Maskhadov has been unable to assert his authority, the country has become a hunting ground for criminal and fundamentalist groups that operate with impunity.

The arrival of Islamic fundamentalist groups known as Wahhabis is one such example. Their arrival was unexpected because they oppose all forms of popular religion, including Sufism, which is dominant in the northern Caucasus. In Chechnya, Islam was established by the Naqshbandiya and Qadiriya Sufi brotherhoods. Identifying with the national resistance movement during the wars of the nineteenth century, these brotherhoods became a central element of Chechen society during the era of Stalinist repression and deportation. Despite its antagonism towards the Sufis, the Wahhabi tradition successfully established itself thanks to the previous war, which profoundly disrupted Chechen society and hardened Chechen attitudes. Although the Wahhabi tradition remains marginal, it has consolidated its influence by offering a framework for socialization to disoriented young people in a devastated country. Fundamentalism did not, however, progress entirely unopposed. When the war ended, the Wahhabis were expelled from many areas, sometimes after armed struggles, as at Gudermes in the summer of 1998. Although the Wahhabis retreated to their strongholds, they continue to exert tremendous influence because of their economic clout. Aided by the blockade imposed by Moscow and the withdrawal of the few humanitarian organizations present in Chechnya, fundamentalist networks have effectively become the only source of external financing in Chechnya.

The Wahhabi groups exhibit considerable potential to destabilize Chechnya, as shown by their armed intervention in neighboring Dagestan. In early August 1999, and again in the following month, Shamil Bassaev and Emir Khattab, a Wahhabi commander of Saudi origin who fought in Chechnya during the last conflict, crossed over to Dagestan with several hundred fighters to assist an Islamic group in the region of Botlikh and Tsumada. This incursion by militant Wahhabis was backed by sponsors from the Middle East and was resisted by Dagestani federal forces. Together with the deadly bomb attacks carried out in Russia in August and September 1999, this military escapade (to which Chechen hard-liners either foolishly committed themselves or into which they allowed themselves to be led) provided the trigger, or the pretext, for Russia's present war against Chechnya.

Prelude to Renewed Conflict

On August 31, 1996, the Khasavyurt Accords, signed by then Prime Minister Alexander Lebed and Aslan Maskhadov following Russia's defeat in Grozny, paved the way for a political resolution. Couched in deliberately ambiguous terms, it gave the warring parties five years to stabilize their relationship and recover from the effects of war. Negotiations followed, and an end to the bewildering cycle of resistance and oppression appeared in sight. On December 31, 1996, the last Russian units left Chechen territory.

One month later, Aslan Maskhadov was elected president of the Chechen Republic of Ichkeria in an election recognized as legitimate both by the Organization for Security and Cooperation in Europe (OSCE) and by the leaders of the Russian Federation. (The official name for the separatist republic, Ichkeria refers to the mountainous region in southern Chechnya that has been the cradle of resistance to Russian expansionism since the 18th century). Finally, on May 12, 1997, Boris Yeltsin and Maskhadov signed a peace accord at the Kremlin. Under the accord, the two parties, "motivated by the desire to end centuries of confrontation," made a commitment to "abandon forever the use of force and the threat to use force in all disputes" and to "maintain mutual relations in accordance with the generally accepted principles and standards of international law." The new agreement seemed to open the door for more peaceful relations and for a settlement on Chechnya's future status.

The talks, however, broke down. The Chechens were convinced that their military victory earned them the right to political independence, while the Russians insisted on regarding Chechnya as a part of the Russian Federation. In the new Russian government formed under Sergei Kiriyenko, nobody was put in charge of relations with Chechnya. By March 1998, negotiations had reached an impasse even before they had really begun.

The election of Aslan Maskhadov testified to the aspirations of a people weary of war. They expected their president to normalize relations with Russia, to win international recognition for the Chechen republic, and to obtain the funds needed to rebuild the country and kick-start the economy. Moscow did not make this task easy, leaving Maskhadov with no concrete results and no room to maneuver. His position grew weaker with respect to Shamil Basayev and Chechen partisans hostile to Russia. The prospects for peace grew increasingly dim.

Russia's Revenge

On October 1, 1999, after subjecting the villages close to the Dagestan border to three weeks of intensive bombing, the Russian army went on the offensive and penetrated Chechen territory. Russia's Prime Minister Vladimir Putin refused to recognize the legitimacy of Chechen President Aslan Maskhadov, and federal forces moved to create a "security zone" by occupying the Chechen districts of Naurskaya and Shelkovskaya—traditionally regarded as the least hostile to Russia. Russia initially appeared content to establish a cordon sanitaire and to bomb alleged terrorist bases. Two weeks later, however, the federal army crossed the Terek River, declared its intention to "destroy armed bands throughout the territory," and began its march on Grozny.

Meanwhile, Vladimir Putin declared that his military objective was the "reconquest of Chechnya." This policy shift reflected the irrational Kremlin decision-making process. Today, as in 1994, the fate of Chechnya is in the hands of irresponsible politicians who understand only the language of force and who are incapable of proposing a model for a balanced relationship between Moscow and the countries that made up the former Soviet empire.

This time, however, there is a difference. The Russian people, who in 1994 opposed the "Kremlin's war" against Chechnya, now wholeheartedly support Putin's intransigence. Even politicians regarded as "liberals" in the West dare not question this vast outpouring of patriotic fervor, fueled by a media machine manipulated by political authorities and ridden with racist and xenophobic overtones. Even though most Russians admit that Chechnya is not Russia, they see Chechen independence as a violation of Russian territorial integrity. Russia is thus defending borders within its own territory in what Georges Charachidzé calls a "war of independence in reverse."

In the current conflict, the army's role is clearer than it was in December 1994, when it was sent to "reestablish constitutional order" in Chechnya and from the outset found itself confronted with civilian protests. Reluctantly drawn into a campaign of repression, the Russian army—ill-prepared, badly organized, and low in morale—was forced to improvise. Today, Russian generals display no scruples about intervening militarily on territory they regard as part of the Russian Federation. The time is long gone when military leaders such as General Boris Gromov either voiced their opposition or resigned. Today, the generals in charge of military operations, including Anatoly Kvashnin, Vladimir Shamanov, and Konstantin Pulikovsky, are all veterans of the previous campaign and are eager to avenge the humiliation of their 1996 defeat. We have come a long way from the ambiguities of the "simple policing operation" of the winter of 1994. War has now been engaged in earnest by leaders who intend to make it total and final. Chechnya is plainly regarded as a territory to reconquer. Gas and electricity have been cut off, a measure not taken during the last conflict. The question of the use of force has also been immediately resolved. During the last conflict the army became accustomed to shooting at civilians. As the summer progressed, federal forces gradually massed around the separatist republic and now number 100,000. Since the bombing of Chechnya began on September 5, 1999, those forces have made extensive use of every means at their disposal: bomber planes, heavy artillery, and even surface-to-surface missiles, which were not used to a large extent three years ago. Nor do Russian forces now rule out the use of new weapons of mass destruction, euphemistically described as "non-orthodox" by their military leaders.

Total War

From the first days of the conflict, massive, indiscriminate bombing caused hundreds of thousands of civilians to flee. One hundred fifty thousand managed to find refuge in neighboring Ingushetia until the army seized control of the border at the end of October. Since then, the exodus has slowed to a trickle; border crossings are now very rare. Most of the population has now made its way back to the mountains of southern Chechnya in a frantic bid to escape the Russian steamroller. But the mountains have become a dead end, subject to constant airplane and helicopter fire concentrated in particular on the last remaining road out of Chechnya: the trail that crosses the Caucasus in the direction of Georgia. There is no sanctuary. Chechnya has become a giant human trap in which over half a million displaced people wander back and forth, desperate to escape the bombing.

When this war of destruction with long-distance weapons eventually gives way to "cleansing operations," the key factor will be the extent to which the generals can occupy the towns while limiting abuses by their soldiers. Given the weaknesses in the chain of command and the erratic discipline among Russian troops, there is a significant risk that the Russian federal forces will again indulge in an orgy of pillaging and massacre. During the last war, "liberated" towns were the setting for large-scale abuses: thousands of men disappeared into "filtration camps" where they were subject to terror and arbitrary mistreatment. There are already persistent reports of arbitrary arrests and summary executions. The situation in Chechnya is beginning to resemble a pogrom. If these murderous practices were to become more widespread, the Chechens would have no choice but to take up arms and the federal forces would again find themselves trapped in a deadly spiral of vengeance and indiscriminate reprisals.

The Chimera of Pacification

The problems raised by the occupation of Chechnya's towns foreshadow the difficulties to come. Apart from waging a war of destruction, the strategy of the Russian army appears unlikely to offer anything that might normalize the situation. Here, too, the experience of the last war highlights the flaws in Russia's approach. Three years ago, just as in the 19th century, the Russian military proved incapable of successfully implementing a colonial policy. In the absence of any genuine understanding of Chechen society, Russia's military operations have always lacked a convincing political rationale. Just as Russia's leaders have always described the Chechens as primitive beings, cunning and criminal, they have always perceived Chechen society as traditional, fixed, and fragmented. These prejudices partly explain Russia's inability to comprehend the Chechen condition and Russia's persistence in waging war and imposing its colonial policy.

Russia's leaders believe that comprehending Chechnya's clan system is key to understanding Chechen society. Typical of colonial ethnography, this approach has always led Russians to exaggerate the unchangeable and rigid nature of a society that has in fact been profoundly transformed by a number of political traumas, the most significant of which was deportation. Their approach has also led them to underestimate the political dynamics and particularly the power of the nationalist movement, which is a phenomenon both too "modern" to be integrated into the "tribal" model and too ideologically uncomfortable to be acknowledged without revealing Moscow's imperialist strategy. The Russians' tendency to exaggerate the significance of clan divisions explains the failure of their policies of division, which were designed to turn the Chechen conflict into an Afghanistan-type campaign by fomenting a "clan war." The divisions in Chechen society are certainly very real, as demonstrated by the Chechen leaders' obsessive fear of a possible civil war. But they are more political than clan based, and Moscow's clumsy, brutal attempts to divide the country have most often had the effect of unifying the Chechen people.

If Russia's leaders have never succeeded in undermining the influence and cohesion of the separatists, they have also never been able to convince the Chechen people to accept Moscow's authority. During the last war, it was clear to all observers that Russia's so-called "pacification" strategies were erratic and often quite absurd. Even villages reputed to be "pro-Russian" or those that had signed peace accords were bombed, attacked, or pillaged; cooperation with federal forces never offered a guarantee of safety. This time the eyewitness accounts gathered by Western journalists in the officially pacified "security zone" to the north of the Terek River testify to the brutality of federal forces and the climate of suspicion and hostility that reigns in Chechnya.

Russian soldiers have become prisoners of their own propaganda. Their traditional aggression toward the Chechen people is being exacerbated by their erratic discipline. Some units have been manipulating the war on their own while others simply run amok. It is Chechen civilians who must deal with the bloody consequences. Spurred on by their own fears and a healthy supply of vodka, soldiers indulge in pillaging, racketeering, and indiscriminate fighting. The same errors have been repeated throughout history. Moscow's political options are again receding behind empty promises to pay salaries or pensions and the repeated blunders of its federal forces. Today, just as in the 19th century, Russian troops control only that part of Chechnya in which they happen to be at the time and seem to compensate for their feelings of powerlessness by engaging in acts of violence. In the absence of a coherent policy, the Russians are condemned to try repeatedly to reconquer a population which, though weary of war, is radicalized again and again by the brutality of occupation.

Further limiting the prospects for normalization is the fact that Moscow has no political solution to offer that might convince the Chechens to share the destiny of the Russians. During the last war, the pro-Russian Chechen administration was never able to win the slightest legitimacy, and the reappearance of one of its members, Beslan Gantemirov—now being touted as "the only legitimate authority on Chechen territory"—shows how limited Moscow's options are. Gantemirov is a former mayor of Grozny, who was in charge of reconstruction programs in the last war. Jailed for embezzlement, he was then hastily summoned from his prison cell in November 1999 to be hailed by Boris Yeltsin as the "representative of the Chechen people." Unless he wants to lose all credibility, no Chechen leader dares to compromise the republic's independence. The Kremlin may well have trouble finding a successor to Aslan Maskhadov, whose legitimacy it deliberately undermined on the first day of the armed intervention. The Kremlin would clearly find it much easier to reverse its position on Maskhadov than to gain even the slightest degree of credibility for the puppet regime it seeks to install.

Searching for Solutions

It is clear that war will not help Moscow achieve any of the objectives it declared at the onset of hostilities. Far from bringing Chechnya back into the Russian Federation, the latest war only intensifies the feelings of suspicion and hostility that have built up over two centuries of confrontation. Far from weakening the hard-liners, the war cannot fail to harden the attitudes of the Chechen people and strengthen the cause of those who favor all-out war with Russia. Consequently, Russia's only solution is negotiation. Sooner or later, Russia must return to the negotiating table. Unfortunately, this war has little to do with Russia's declared goals in Chechnya, and the decision-making process at the Kremlin is so tortuous that it defies all reason. All democratic nations must try to convince Moscow that it is in its own interest to find a political solution to the conflict.

Western leaders finally understand the ambiguous nature of Russia's "democratic transition" and are grasping the absurdity of offering unconditional support for Russian policy. Faced with the alarming policy shifts of the "New Russia" and with Russia's potential to destabilize the Caucasus, democratic nations at last seem ready to remind Russia of the values to which they themselves lay claim.

The West would do well to translate this new firmness into realistic and credible pressure, aimed at encouraging Russian leaders to call a cease-fire and find a political solution to the conflict. Perhaps the best way to achieve this would be to target Russian leaders' personal investments in the West. Such measures would, in any case, be more effective than empty rhetoric and moralizing, since Russia's present leaders are past masters at the art of flattering national pride by encouraging a pan-Russian and anti-Western nationalism.

Even if Moscow were to realize that it is in its own interest to search for a political solution to the conflict, it would find it hard to back out now. Even back in August 1996, when it was mired in war, Russia seemed unable to end the bloodbath until Alexander Lebed, amid power struggles at the Kremlin, managed, as his final act, to commit his country to the search for a negotiated solution. The way out of the current crisis will again be dependent upon electoral affairs, financial scandals, alliances within the circles of power, and a host of other factors only marginally related to Chechnya or the Caucasus.

Even supposing the Russians decide to commit themselves to the search for a negotiated solution, it would not be easy for those negotiations to begin. After all, with whom are the Chechens to negotiate? On the Chechen side, Aslan Maskhadov is still a legitimate negotiating partner, even if he is not totally in control of the situation. On the Russian side, on the other hand, there are few trustworthy negotiating partners. How can the Chechens trust a regime that every three years subjects its population to indiscriminate bombing with weapons of massive destruction?

Western nations have an essential role to play in helping Russia out of the morass. Even if Chechnya were an internal Russian affair, democratic nations cannot possibly remain passive in the face of this conflict. The means being employed are simply unacceptable and in violation both of the "demands of public conscience" and of Russia's obligations as a member of the OSCE, the Council of Europe, and the United Nations. If unchecked, the fighting in Chechnya threatens to destabilize the entire Caucasus region while spelling disaster for the Russian people and their political system.

Section Three
International Aid

CHAPTER TWELVE
Life, Death, and Aid

Originally published in English as the introduction to *Life, Death, and Aid: The Médecins Sans Frontières Report on World Crisis Intervention*, Routledge/Hachette 1993

The United Nations, powerless during the Cold War as a result of the superpower hostility that essentially restricted its role to development aid, has now been given a real ability to take initiative and is looking to develop its capability for emergency interventions in crisis situations.

The end of the Cold War raised again the idea of an international system based on shared values, administered by international institutions, and defended by democratic countries. Wars are no longer considered inevitable. In the face of the increasing number of crises, the international community is regularly called upon to encourage negotiations, to interpose itself between factions, and to assist people at risk. Although for years the great powers were vilified for exacerbating and protracting conflicts throughout the world, today all hopes are pinned on their involvement.

A New Role for the United Nations
The United Nations' return to center stage, symbolized by the award of the Nobel Peace Prize to the Blue Helmets in 1988, can be seen in the frenetic increase in its activity. In the four years from 1988 to 1992, it has carried out more operations—13 in all—than in the preceding 40 years and the number of Blue Helmets has increased from 10,000 to 52,000. Since then, the United Nations has continued to grow. By June 1993, the number of Blue Helmets had increased to 75,000, mainly owing to the intervention in Somalia, and no month goes by without a new operation starting up—in Rwanda, Georgia, Tajikistan, or South Africa.

This boom in UN activity is in striking contrast to its past inertia. East-West confrontation paralyzed the Security Council for 40 years and prevented the implementation of the collective security system provided for by the San Francisco Charter. The United Nations could not do much about the new conflicts springing up in the shadow of superpower rivalry. It was limited to intervening at the fringe of conflicts, in what was to become known as "peacekeeping." This improvised mechanism, which was not foreseen under the charter and which Secretary-General Dag Hammarskjöld described as "chapter six and a half," bridged the gap between Chapter VI, dealing with the peaceful resolution of conflicts, and Chapter VII, covering a whole range of constraints to be used if peaceful methods failed, ranging from economic sanctions to the use of force.

The essential elements of peacekeeping—the agreement of opposing sides to the deployment of Blue Helmets and the nonuse of force, except in the last resort and in case of self-defense—clearly reflected the constraints involved in playing the Cold War game. This meant, in effect, the deployment of observers or neutral forces between the warring parties, providing they had agreed to suspend hostilities in the first place. Essentially, this did little more than preserve the status quo and win time until a political solution, however unlikely, could be found.

Today, the observers have become players. The permanent members of the Security Council, who used and abused their right of veto for four decades, have finally begun to collaborate in the spirit of collegiality laid out in the charter and are ready to play the game of multilateral diplomacy. The number of interventions has increased, as has the diversity of UN missions. As a result, peacekeeping has become a hazier concept, now covering a whole range of activities from mine clearing to organizing elections, demobilizing and disarming combatants, repatriating and reintegrating refugees, training police forces, defending human rights, and rebuilding ruined economies.

The operations in 1990–91 in Angola, El Salvador, and Cambodia were among the first illustrations of this newly extended field of intervention—albeit improvised in a way that has characterized peacekeeping since its inception. It is obvious, however, that these recent interventions have broken away from the traditional recipe based on the deployment of Blue Helmets with the agreement of the combatants following a cease-fire or peace agreement. UN operations no longer aim solely at maintaining the status quo, as can be seen in its 1992 interventions in Bosnia and Somalia. Concern for stability has not diminished—indeed, it is stronger than ever—but it is accompanied by a more dynamic interpretation of the role of the United Nations, as it is entrusted not only with peacekeeping as such but also the protection of humanitarian aid operations. The United Nations' role has never been so important—nor has it ever been so controversial.

Sovereignty and Intervention

Against this new background, the foundations of the United Nations appear all the more anachronistic. One of the major problems is that the UN intervention system is based on the sovereignty principle. Chapter II(7) of the UN charter stresses that a country's internal affairs are its exclusive concern. Although civil wars and internal strife account for most present-day conflicts, the charter does not touch on internal problems. As a result, the mechanisms for collective security are, in principle, applicable only in international conflicts.

Today however, this supremacy of the nation-state, which was reaffirmed at the end of World War II, strengthened during the decolonization period, and frozen by East-West confrontation, has become outdated. The end of the Cold War has had the dual effect of questioning the Yalta world order, sustained by the ideological blocs, and the principle of territorial sovereignty enshrined in the treaty of Westphalia.

The idea of the nation-state was already put into question in the '70s, before the fall of the Berlin Wall began to show its first effects. The Helsinki Agreements eroded the principle of sovereignty by turning human rights into an issue of supranational concern. Many countries had long lost faith in it anyway, their authoritarian rulers having discredited it beyond redemption.

Since then, it has continually been challenged. As the economies of the world have become increasingly integrated, so too have many other spheres, such as the media, the environment, migrations, and humanitarian aid. Even the most repressive states have lost the ability to control the circulation of people and ideas. By contrast, the United Nations' respect for sovereignty makes it look like a bastion of tradition.

The human rights movement at the end of the '80s prompted further attacks on sovereignty. The idea that regimes can commit large-scale

84

human rights violations with impunity had become unacceptable, as was evidenced by UN Secretary-General Javier Perez de Cuellar at the end of his term of office, who claimed there was "an irresistible change in public opinion" in favor of the defense of human rights, which must prevail both on our borders and in international law. His opinion was reiterated by his successor, Boutros Boutros-Ghali, who also believes that "the time of absolute and exclusive sovereignty is over."

Respect for sovereignty remains all important, but in some instances calls for the protection of victims seem to have been heeded. Seen from that angle, there are common interventionist overtones in Security Council Resolution 688 condemning Iraq's repression of its civilian population—and insisting that humanitarian organizations have immediate access to them—, Resolution 770 on the protection of humanitarian convoys in Bosnia, and, finally, Resolution 794 on the use of force to restore security for aid operations in Somalia.

Each of these three resolutions on Iraq, Bosnia, and Somalia are landmarks in the recent history of international intervention. While self-defense used to provide the only justification for intervention in an internal conflict—the Tanzanian intervention in Uganda and the Vietnamese invasion of Cambodia were presented in 1979 as a reply to outside aggression—humanitarian concerns are now put forward as the one key reason for intervention. Resolution 688 on Iraq was a first in that it considered the repression of a civilian population a threat to international peace and security in the form of the mass exodus of refugees into neighboring countries.

In Resolutions 770 on Bosnia and 794 on Somalia, which opened the way to interventions authorizing the use of force, in conformity with Chapter VII of the charter, it is the crisis itself that was described as a threat to peace and security. Although the UN troops in Croatia took on a conventional peacekeeping mission—in fact guaranteeing the status quo in areas captured by Serbs—those who were finally deployed in the open war of Bosnia, after much procrastination, were called on to use "all necessary means" to protect humanitarian convoys.

Similarly, in Somalia, the United Nations went from sending, almost discreetly, 50 observers and 500 Blue Helmets with the warlords' consent, to the non-negotiated deployment of 2,500 extra troops. This was followed by the landing of 30,000 GIs authorized to "employ all necessary means to ensure security for humanitarian aid operations," and finally, to the high-handed takeover of the country by 28,000 Blue Helmets, ready—and often willing—to use force. The operations carried out in 1992 demonstrate the emergence, still hesitant and cautious in Bosnia, but more obvious and aggressive in Somalia, of new kinds of intervention that are further removed from the traditional principles of peacekeeping.

At Pains to Handle Internal Crises

Despite these recent developments, caution remains the rule. The Security Council is still reluctant to consider even large-scale humanitarian violations as threats to peace and international security. However, decades of Cold War constraints and strict observance of noninterference alone cannot explain the present inability to act. The international community has obvious difficulty in acting in internal crises, usually quite complex and not susceptible to resolution by outside intervention. The United Nations can certainly play a vital role as arbitrator and guarantor when the warring parties agree to negotiate peace, but in the absence of such an agreement, outside intervention can become part of the problem as much as it can bring a long-term solution—as was the case in the Congo from 1960 to 1964 and Lebanon from 1982 to 1984, where the international forces rapidly became parties to the conflicts.

The international community is confronted with three types of crises: wars of aggression (Kuwait), large-scale human rights violations and repression of minorities (Burma), and the total collapse of law and order (Somalia). In none of these cases are there any easy answers, but the United Nations is aware it must be ready to commit itself to the long and painstaking search for long-term solutions.

More importantly, the United Nations is obviously at pains to catch up with an ever changing, seemingly chaotic world, where institutions are crumbling, armed forces are splitting up into factions, and conflicts are tearing entire countries apart. Deprived of their former Cold War backers, both government forces and guerilla movements in today's war spots are increasingly left to fend for themselves and forced to fight over the scant resources available.

Obliged to depend on their own strength, they have to find new, and often brutal, ways of procuring weapons and consolidating power.

The majority of wars today have become "privatized" concerns, financed by looting, racketeering, and trafficking. The striking feature common to most present-day crisis situations is self-perpetuation of violence. It is true that the end of the Cold War opened new opportunities for negotiated solutions, but it has also lessened the possibilities for powerful countries to exert real pressure on the warring parties. Moreover, as trustworthy representatives and leaders are harder to find on the scenes of today's conflicts, it is all the more difficult to impose respect for international law. Laws that cannot be enforced only pave the way for lawlessness. To add to this atmosphere of fragmentation, member countries are not respecting their financial commitments to the United Nations as they can no longer see any direct return on their investment.

How Best to Intervene?

Whatever the difficulties in intervening, the United Nations is faced with an irrepressible demand for action, but many questions remain open as to how best to intervene. No doubt, the one condition for success is early involvement. In this regard, the developments of the past years reveal large gaps in the international community's ability to curtail the spiral of violence at an early stage before it spins entire societies into self-destruction. In the absence of international involvement, the Liberian conflict developed over six months into a frenzy of violence and massacres before a regional force intervened. In Somalia, the international community took almost two years to react, after having left the country prey to violence and starvation. In the former Yugoslavia, the European Community hesitated, leaving the field free for the aggressors to pursue a policy of terror and "ethnic cleansing" in the heart of Europe. From the Caucasus to Tajikistan, from Zaire to Rwanda, the so-called policies of prevention are in fact mainly reactive and, more often than not, too late.

Consequently, the most pressing question too often concerns that of the last resort solution—military intervention. Although stepping in without the agreement of the warring parties is becoming more and more common, the United Nations is still ill prepared to deal with the situation.

Its ill-defined mandates and blatant shortcomings in coordinating various national contingents have seriously damaged its credibility and weakened the deterrent effect of the armed forces placed under its banner.

The UN aid agencies, too, have to improve their operational efficiency. Despite vague attempts at reform, the United Nations continues to be governed by inertia, lack of accountability, sometimes even outright incompetence, which has diminished its ability to respond, especially to emergencies. Above all, improved coordination between the different UN bodies is long overdue. The machinery is grinding to a halt as the myriad UN agencies continue to function autonomously like private fiefdoms while the United Nations has to juggle peacekeeping, emergency relief, and long-term recovery programs all at once. In fairness however, the United Nations' ability to intervene ultimately depends on the political and financial backing of the member states, particularly in the West. Boutros-Ghali is probably right in saying that what cripples the organization most is too-high expectations.

In the post–Cold War world, it is the countries of the West, led by the United States, which find themselves, by default, guarantors of the world order, although they are reluctant to act as an international police force. In the Gulf War, the United Nations launched its biggest operation since the intervention in Korea to reestablish Kuwait's international borders, yet the coalition forces did nothing to defend the Shiites or the Kurds when they were violently suppressed by Baghdad. It took the mass exodus across the frontiers of neighboring countries to provoke an international intervention, which turned out to be little more than an after-sales service forced on the participants in order to safeguard the image of a "just war." It responded to public emotion and removed the threat of a massive influx of refugees into Turkey.

This half-hearted commitment to the Iraqi Kurds illustrates the firm resolve of UN member states to maintain the status quo. Faced with many crisis situations throughout the world, democratic countries are torn between defending human rights, i.e., contemplating intervention, and their reluctance to run the risks involved. The Security Council reflects the way the balance has tilted when it churns out resolutions without giving itself the means to enforce them.

The developments of the past two years have shattered all illusions of the coherent system of international protection that was supposedly heralded in Iraqi Kurdistan. More calls for help can be heard from oppressed people and minority groups, but Western countries have neither the financial and military clout, nor, above all, the political will to impose a new world order based on respect for human rights. The international community's response will only be prompted by political interests, media visibility, and the sustained pressure of public opinion.

In short, Part One of *Life, Death, and Aid* examines the four levels of international involvement in crisis situations: complete absence from the scene of forgotten tragedies, intervention by regional powers, peacemaking missions, and military interventions on humanitarian grounds.

1. Nonintervention

For over a year, the highly publicized UN operations in Bosnia, Somalia, and Cambodia have overshadowed the lack of commitment to many other countries torn apart by war. Admittedly, these countries are not totally forgotten as humanitarian organizations and UN agencies struggle to bring aid to people at risk despite insecurity and political obstacles. More often than not, international intervention is restricted to timid diplomatic overtures in these countries and, eventually, to economic pressures, but this does not guarantee genuine access to victims or an end to human rights violations. In Sudan and Afghanistan, the international community failed miserably to ensure that regular aid reached the threatened populations because it lacked real political commitment. Sudan, however, remains the harshest illustration of what amounts to "non-assistance to populations in danger."

2. Regional Intervention

The United Nations has been faced with so many requests for help over the past few years that the secretary-general has been trying to encourage a more significant role for regional organizations in putting UN resolutions into force, in accordance with Chapter VIII of the charter. However, the problem has been to find credible partners. Many regional organizations are limited by a lack of ability, resources, or political cohesion from taking part in peacekeeping operations. An example of this was the powerlessness of the Organization of African Unity (OAU) to deal either with the Somalia tragedy or any of the other recurring crises on the continent. However, the Organization of American States (OAS) and the European Economic Community (EEC) have demonstrated a degree of cooperation with the United Nations, albeit with limited success, in Haiti and the former Yugoslavia.

Regional interventions have an obvious advantage in that they bring together the countries directly concerned and most likely to intervene; but their interests may not be purely altruistic: they do not always wait for the United Nations' invitation before interfering with their neighbors' problems. Syria intervened in Lebanon in 1976 under the guise of the "Arab Dissuasion Force" and, by playing a role akin to a pyromaniac fireman, succeeded in strengthening its grip on the country until its role was legitimized by the Taif Agreements. In 1971 India intervened and precipitated the secession of its Pakistani rival by taking advantage of the large-scale human rights violations in East Pakistan and the arrival of millions of refugees across its borders. India, again, benefited from its regional supremacy in 1987, when it intervened in Sri Lanka, on the pretext of bringing humanitarian aid to the Tamils. As for Vietnam's intervention in Cambodia in 1979, it put an end to the Khmer Rouge campaign of extermination, but in essence it ensured Hanoi's domination of the Indo-Chinese peninsula.

There are many such ambiguities in the regional interventions launched over the past years. In Tajikistan, Russia, which controls the only organized armed forces in the republic, can hardly qualify as a peace guarantor as Moscow played a determining role in the communists' return to power. Ironically, Russia was readily given its peacekeeper credentials by an international community unwilling to get bogged down in the forgotten conflict. The deployment of a "mixed intervention force" in Ossetia and Abkhazia can hardly hide the central policing role played by Russia in the Caucasus conflicts. Here, Moscow has taken on the dual role of referee and player in its efforts to maintain its influence in the region, while looking for international backing.

Finally, Nigeria, which is the main backer of the West African intervention force in Liberia, argues, with the United Nations' blessing, that peace can only be attained by the use of force. Famine relief operations are hampered in the process, but then aid is in turn accused of hindering "peace efforts."

3. Peacemaking Operations

The end of the Cold War has opened up the possibility of resolving conflicts born in the shadow of superpower rivalry at the end of the 1970s. But these conflicts have deep local roots, structured around war economies that tend to perpetuate themselves, roots that go deeper than political and ideological differences.

In Central America, southern Africa and Southeast Asia, the former superpowers are involved in peace negotiations with UN help, with the special role of supervising their application in the field. In El Salvador, Angola, Cambodia, and, more recently, Mozambique, the United Nations has intervened to guarantee cease-fires, oversee disarmament, repatriate refugees, organize elections, and rebuild infrastructures, etc. The success of such large-scale operations requires reliable support from member states at a time when the United Nations is in serious financial difficulties. It also requires effective coordination between the individual, but necessarily interdependent, partners in these complex operations.

However, the principal problem relates to the difficulty in turning a diplomatic agreement into a political process. In this sense, with the exception of El Salvador, the United Nations has always behaved as if its only objective was to organize the elections on a fixed date. Successful peacemaking requires a much broader interpretation of the UN mandate, as Angola and Cambodia have learned to their cost.

4. Military Interventions with Humanitarian Aims

Further up the scale of intervention, humanitarian considerations have been pushed into the foreground in order to justify armed intervention in the face of a repressive regime (Iraq), a state under attack (Bosnia), or a collapsing system (Somalia). At first glance, there is no reason not to welcome this new international willingness to intervene, but putting good intentions into effect is a tricky task. Intervention in internal conflicts, without the agreement of the opposing sides, means that the international force can either favor negotiations at the risk of being taken hostage by one side or another, or it can opt for force and risk becoming yet another party to the conflict. The operations launched in 1992 are evidence of the difficulty of such interventions, characterized as they are by impotence in Bosnia, where humanitarian aid has done more to help than to hinder "ethnic cleansing," and by aggression in Somalia, where it was soon sidelined by sheer military might.

In both cases, the problem has been exacerbated by the absence of a clear political objective. In Bosnia, the humanitarian effort initially served as an alibi for the West's standoff in the face of aggression before becoming another, more perverse, argument against military action, which might endanger troops deployed in the field. In Somalia, the use of force in a political vacuum made humanitarian aid one of the first casualties of war. In order to achieve a quick military victory over the Somali factions, the Blue Helmets have cast aside all pretense of impartiality and independence, attacking hospitals and aid organizations. In doing so, they have discredited the entire international relief effort.

This peace enforcement mission, the first ever for the United Nations, throws a particularly harsh light on the contradictions between the restoration of peace, which supposes a clearly defined political strategy, and humanitarian aid, which demands strict neutrality. We hope that the UN impasse in Bosnia and Somalia will force a much-needed political debate on the principles and workings of future international interventions.

CHAPTER THIRTEEN

Europe, Refugees, and War

Originally published in *Le front du refuge. Réfugiés, exilés, demandeurs d'asile: citoyens?*
ed. Dominique Nalpas, De la Démocratie, Bruxelles, 1994, p.97-112

With the world in its present state of upheaval, refugees are a tragic per-
sonification of global turmoil. Their plight speaks to wartime conditions
everywhere, to famine or oppression that throws millions of uprooted persons onto the highways of exile. However inaccessible the country, however obscure the conflict, floods of refugees inevitably bring it into view
of the international public. In 1992, once more, hundreds of thousands
of Somalis, Sudanese, Tajiks, Burmese Rohingyas, Serbs, Croats, Bosnian
Muslims, and more brought the number of refugees throughout the world
to 18 million, according to current censuses; in the same year the number
of persons displaced within their own country rose to 20 million.

Developments over recent months constitute a scathing rebuttal to the
once fondly held notion that the Cold War's end might yield a solution to
the persistent question of refugees. In 1989 the collapse of the Berlin Wall
under the pressure of asylum seekers fostered hope for a solution: the end
of totalitarianism seemed to proclaim that Russians, Poles, or Romanians
eager for freedom would have merely to knock at the door of Western
countries. Likewise, the end of East-West antagonism held out the possibility of resolving conflicts ignited in a climate of ideological confrontation
and dangled the hope that millions of refugees stagnating in camps since
the 1970s would return to their countries of origin.

For a brief period even the concept of "refugee" seemed to become
indistinct. Overlooking conflicts in the Southern Hemisphere, Europe
suddenly viewed all of its Eastern neighbors with apprehension. Red
Army tanks were soon displaced on the short list of collective fears by the
spectre of a vast migration of the suffering that, in the fall of 1990, looked
to be a veritable tidal wave. In an overwrought media environment,
the figure of the migrant replaced that of the dissident in the Western

imagination, and the right to circulate freely, long upheld by democratic nations, yielded to the fear of invasion. But in short order the nations of Europe would be confronted with the tragic reality—mass exoduses provoked by war and peril. Somalia, Burma, and especially the ex-Yugoslavia would abruptly remind the public that, behind the nightmare fantasy of Europe submerged in a wave of immigration, real tragedies were unfolding in a climate of rising religious and ethnic identification, heightened animosities, and an explosion of nationalist sentiment.

In their violence and agitation, these wrenching, identity-based cleavages mark the collapse of two orders: the Communist system to the east (imposed) and the new world order (abortive). The set of problems posed by refugees changed after the dissolution of the Eastern bloc and the break-up of Yugoslavia. It would have been startling if this overall phenomenon—at the nexus of border controversies, conflicts, and migration flows—had been unaffected by resurgent nations, seething unrest amongst minorities, or decaying economies. Far from subsiding, conflicts are growing in number—far from dropping, the number of asylum seekers increases with no end in sight. Suddenly, the reality of forced exoduses is once again a feature of the landscape of migration—a looming feature that defies solution by European refugee policy and poses fresh questions for the system of international refugee protection.

The Three Ages of Refugees

The international system for the protection of refugees came into being after the Second World War with the signing of the 1951 convention on the status of refugees and the creation of the UN High Commissioner for Refugees (UNHCR). The convention defined as a refugee any person who, "…owing to well-founded fear of being persecuted for reasons of race, religion, nationality, membership of a particular social group or political opinion, is outside the country of his nationality and is unable, or owing to such fear, is unwilling to avail himself of the protection of that country…." This definition, based on an individual-case approach focusing on discrimination or persecution, was very much a reflection of Europe's preoccupations at a time when it was still experiencing the ripple effects of Nazi oppression and already menaced by the Soviet system. In fact, by the start of the 1950s, the majority of the nearly 30 million persons displaced by the war had already been resettled, Europe had been permanently divided into two opposed blocs, and, in the Cold War context, refugees were seen in the same light as dissidents. Most refugees were fleeing totalitarian regimes and seeking asylum in democratic countries. The preferred solution at the time was permanent resettlement in Europe or the United States with legal rights and a status similar to those enjoyed by nationals in the host country. Asylum policies in Western countries were all the more generous because refugees were viewed positively in the context of the Cold War. They were "choosing freedom" and assimilated easily into their host countries because the countries they came from were of the same cultural fabric. Up until the end of the 1950s, in fact, the refugee problem was for the most part an intra-European question, consisting primarily of East- West migration. The 1951 convention—ostensibly universal—in reality applied only to Europe. It was not until 1967 and the New York protocol that the mandate of UNHCR extended to the rest of the world.

Starting in the 1960s, struggles for independence and internal conflicts within the newly independent African and Asian states touched off large flows of refugees. After the decolonization movements, the UNHCR, together with other UN organizations and the World Bank, turned its attention to the third world and was forced to adjust to a new reality of predominantly South-South migration flows and mass exoduses triggered by war and insecurity. In contrast to the dissidents from beyond the Berlin Wall—victims of repression who appeared at the doorways of Western nations on an individual basis—Southern Hemisphere refugees were collectively fleeing conflict situations and widespread disturbances and usually sought temporary refuge in a neighboring country. For this reason the UN General Assembly expanded the UNHCR's mandate to allow it to deal with large-scale exoduses, and the definition of refugees as persecuted individuals was broadened, de facto, to include collective victims of violence.[1] This

---

[1] Aristide R. Zolberg identifies three categories of refugees: the *activist*, pursued by reason of their political activities; the *target*, persecuted because they belong to a particular group; and the *victim* of violence, fleeing war and insecurity. Only the first two categories are formally recognized in the 1951 definition. Aristide R. Zolberg, *Escape From Violence* (Oxford University Press, 1989).

broadened definition was to a certain extent formalized in the Organization of African Unity convention of 1969 (OAU convention) and in the 1984 Cartagena declaration granting refugee status to any person fleeing war and insecurity.[2] The international community's response to massive third world migrations was primarily humanitarian, in the form of aid to refugees grouped in camps and waiting for the situation in their countries of origin to improve enough to allow for their safe return.

The problem of Southern Hemisphere refugees, long overshadowed by the image of the dissident, was never really brought home to the Western public until the end of the 1970s, when the lengthening shadow of the Cold War reached the third world. The episode of boat people signaled this change in perception. The flight of the Vietnamese, even more so than the Bengali exodus widely covered by the media in 1971, seemed a revelation: Southern Hemisphere refugees, abruptly captured in the news spotlight, sprang into Western public awareness. Media coverage, combined with vivid memories of the Vietnam War and, in the United States, a special sense of responsibility, lent this drama an iconic dimension. On TV screens across the globe, boat people became emblematic victims—victimized by war, by totalitarianism, by pirates, by the China Sea, etc. There was an outpouring of sympathy together with an unprecedented response on the part of Western nations. The boat people were welcomed with open arms, and Southern Hemisphere refugees assumed a prominent place on the international agenda. That the boat people's exodus took place in the context of the end of détente, heightened East-West tensions, and a mounting number of "peripheral" conflicts made the response that much more intense. From Afghanistan to Central America, in Southeast Asia and the Horn of Africa, millions of refugees were suddenly present to

---

[2] Article I, paragraph 1 of the OAU Convention defines "refugee" in the same way as the 1951 convention, but paragraph 2 stretches the definition to include "…every person who, owing to external aggression, occupation, foreign domination, or events seriously disturbing public order … is compelled to leave his place of habitual residence in order to seek refuge in another place outside his country of origin or nationality." The Cartagena Declaration is still more explicit; it stipulates that the definition of refugee should go beyond the elements contained in the 1951 convention to apply to "…persons who have fled their country because their lives, safety or freedom have been threatened by generalized violence, foreign aggression, internal conflicts, massive violations of human rights, or other circumstances which have seriously disturbed public order."

attest to the brutalities of war and the deep hardship experienced under communism. These refugees acquired political significance and a positive aura in the climate of an ideological nostalgia that prevailed at the time—when the image of "freedom fighter" supplanted that of the guerilla fighter in the Western imagination. As a result, UNHCR found itself enjoying increased funding, and Western countries launched an increasing number of initiatives in camps set up on the borders of conflict-ridden countries.

Then the Cold War receded into the past, the "Vietnam Syndrome" faded, the intensity of emotion wound down ... The boat people lost political significance, symbolic weight, and media presence.[3] They are now treated on an equal footing with the Albanian boat people sent back into hardship by the Italian authorities or Haitians escorted back into dictatorship by the US Coast Guard, contrary to principles enunciated in the 1951 convention on refugees. The end of East-West confrontation also illuminated the dubious aspects of keeping refugees in camps that had gradually come to be "humanitarian sanctuaries, and a factor in the perpetuation of conflicts."[4] In the camps, guerilla forces gained political legitimacy via their influence over refugee populations and a financial base by means of the aid pouring in, as well as a ready supply of fighters. In time, the chronic, persistent nature of the camps and the prospect of an indefinite prolongation of the humanitarian status quo would prompt new questions regarding to what extent any solution could be found, apart from direct assistance.

Such questions gained urgency as South-North migrations joined those East-West and South-South migrations that were then drawing the vast majority of refugees and still do today. Indeed, since the start of the 1980s, Western countries have had to face steadily growing streams of asylum seekers. Between 1983 and 1991 their number in western European nations went from 70,000 to 550,000. To be sure, of these hundreds of thousands of persons who, in a time of restrictive immigration policy,

---

[3] On the historical evolution of these representations, see François Jean, "Le Fantôme des Réfugiés" [The Spectre of Refugees], *Esprit* (December 1992).

[4] Jean-Christophe Rufin, *Le Piège Humanitaire* [The Humanitarian Trap] (Hachette-Pluriel, 1993).

97

appear every year at Europe's borders, far from all are accorded refugee status. In France, for example, where the number of asylum seekers went from 22,000 to 46,000 between 1983 and 1991, the number of refugees accepted annually has remained virtually the same; the acceptance rate went from over 70 percent to under 20 percent during that same time period. Similarly, these asylum seekers represent only a slight portion of the millions of refugees accepted into camps by Southern Hemisphere countries. Nevertheless, the major increase of asylum seekers in Western countries has provoked far-reaching changes in policy. The certainties of the Cold War have yielded to deep anxiety amid upheavals around the world and fear of migrations. Gone are the days when refugees voted with their feet: their flight—viewed only yesterday as a paean to freedom—is now perceived as out of control. The refugee question, once identified with human rights, is now seen from the perspective of migration pressures, and policies established in recent decades are now in the process of being drastically modified.

From "Lasting Solutions" ...

Both the scale of these migrations and the growing number of asylum seekers have prompted a reexamination of the refugee question. The chronic, persistent nature of the camps reveals the inadequacies of aid policies in Southern Hemisphere countries, and host country reticence signals the limitations of resettlement policies in Northern Hemisphere countries. Since the beginning of the 1980s, the emphasis has been on "underlying causes" and on "lasting solutions" that could be brought to bear on the issue of refugees.[5] The aid-resettlement combination that for more than three decades formed the core of refugee policies has now been replaced by new buzzwords: "prevention" and "repatriation." But, beyond concerns about assistance and protection, the question of causes and solutions itself raises the issue—a political one—of what position the international community should adopt towards repressive regimes and internal conflicts that inspire the principal refugee flows. There can be no

---

[5] Contemporary thinking on the causes of refugee flows has been heavily influenced by the publication of Sadruddin Agha Khan's report for the UN Human Rights Commission: *Study on Human Rights and Mass Exoduses* (UN, 1981).

doubt, in fact, that social conflicts in the modern world have been internationalized—for no other reason than the migrations they trigger—and that they call for collective solutions. It is every bit as clear that the international community's involvement as an honest broker and guarantor is a vital factor in controlling the violence spreading across the world today—and that any international intervention, if it is to be credible, presumes a degree of political will that is highly unlikely, save in exceptional circumstances. Behind a façade of all humanity united around human rights values, which the notion of an "international community" legitimizes, states continue to promote their own interests and defend their sovereignty tooth and nail. In theory, at least, this conflict between "what the public conscience demands" and the principle of noninterference in a state's domestic affairs is more apparent than it is real: Resolution 688 on Iraq establishes a link between domestic repression and international security based precisely on the threat of refugee flows. But this newly lawful type of intervention does not constitute a policy and has not been easy to put into action.

In recent years the United Nations has backed a growing number of efforts to find solutions to conflicts and enable displaced and refugee populations to return to their countries of origin. In Namibia, El Salvador, and Cambodia, hundreds of thousands of refugees have been successfully repatriated under the aegis of the UNHCR. But, whereas in Namibia and El Salvador the repatriation process was eased by the warring parties' willingness to limit their rivalries to the political sphere, in Cambodia it is happening in an atmosphere of uncertainty: the United Nations is powerless as long as the Khmer Rouge refuses to honor the 1991 Paris accords. In Angola as well, the inability of the international community to guarantee true disarmament by the two warring parties opened the door to the violent contestation of election results and renewed fighting. And in Afghanistan the fall of the Najibullah regime was not enough to restore peace. To be sure, hundreds of thousands of Afghans, refugees for many years in Pakistani camps, have returned home. But they have been replaced by thousands of others fleeing the fighting in Kabul, and tens of thousands of Tajikis have become stranded in northern Afghanistan while trying to escape the war and repression ravaging their country. Afghanistan is a remarkable example of self-perpetuating conflicts, born in the shadow of the Cold War, that have assumed a life of their own amid widespread indifference.

As if these conflicts were not enough, new wars are now breaking out, triggering the flight of hundreds of thousands of refugees and displaced persons. In Liberia in 1990, the belated intervention of a West African buffer force failed to prevent the conflict from deteriorating or the exodus of more than 200,000 refugees to neighboring countries. And in Somalia the recent intervention of Western forces could not erase the fact that for a full two years running this country had been abandoned to itself and the law of the gun, causing hundreds of thousands of refugees to flee to Kenya, Yemen, Ethiopia, etc., and millions more to be uprooted inside the country—adrift amid war and famine, searching for the means to survive and some degree of safety. As for the ex-Yugoslavia, European indecision has allowed the conflict to reach unimaginable dimensions. Unable to take a clear stand during the initial fighting in Croatia and Bosnia, Europe relegated itself to the status of impotent bystander while a strategy of territorial conquest and ethnic cleansing generated mass civilian displacement and deportation. The dilemma was particularly acute because population movements were not merely the consequence of war—they were the objective. In short, the conflict stems from a policy of terror aimed at provoking the flight of undesirable groups in order to "cleanse" ethnically mixed regions and to rule over homogeneous territories. As this horrifying scenario of butchery plays out, the Serbs are driven by an implacable determination, Muslims are cast out onto the highways, central Bosnia has become a cage in which uprooted populations shuttle endlessly back and forth, and Europe is today confronted with a flood of refugees.

... To Containment Strategies

Europe's cravenness in the face of the Yugoslavian tragedy illustrates the reluctance of Western countries to involve themselves in internal crises and the problems of minority populations. The end of the Cold War has reopened the question of how "domestic" policy and "foreign" policy interact, and states are struggling to orient themselves to deal with borders they seek both to breech and—still more—to preserve, at one and the same time. The refugee question is a revealing one, in this respect. It is at the nexus of upheavals troubling the planet: it takes root in wrenching internal cleavages that undermine existing political arrangements and emerges along with new migration flows that make a mockery of borders and territories. It is revealing, as well, because states have, for the most part, responded with avoidance, choosing self-protection over intervention. The preventive policies so much discussed at the moment are, in fact, essentially defensive. Instead of acting at the source, Western countries are trying to dam up the flow.

The example of Iraq offers a singular illustration of the international community's concern to avoid any new refugee problem, even if this has meant offering protection—only too temporarily—to groups repatriated to their own countries. Even though Iraq was thoroughly defeated and under international supervision, coalition forces stood by as Kurdish and Shiite uprisings were bloodily put down. But the spectacle on TV screens of an entire people running amok on and streaming over the borders of neighboring countries provoked a crisis intervention by the West. Behind a humanitarian façade, the neatly effective aim of this intervention was essentially to persuade afflicted Kurds to keep away from the Turkish border and return home by offering them temporary protection and humanitarian aid in northern Iraq.

The international response to the Kurdish exodus is probably the consummate example of a new three-part policy of containment based on repatriation, security zones, and humanitarian aid. Ideally, repatriation is probably the best solution, since it is true that indefinite residence in camps is neither humanely acceptable nor politically desirable. But the situation in the country of origin needs to be conducive to the refugees' return, and the international community must assure itself that it is conducted in dignity and safety. From this point of view the growing acceptance of repatriation to countries at war or under repression, such as Haiti or Burma, raises critical questions that are not likely to be resolved by ephemeral security zones or the provision of temporary aid.

The transition to a political approach, which implies a search for lasting solutions, has in practice meant sticking strictly to humanitarian measures repackaged to appear as intervention. All indications are that the "intervention" so much discussed at present consists solely of moving refugee camps back inside crisis-ridden countries into zones neutralized by an international presence and sustained by aid convoys. This is why the UNHCR's mandate was enlarged de facto, allowing it to intervene in conflict-ridden countries to support a repatriation process or deliver aid on-site to displaced populations about to pour over international borders. This new policy is beginning to be widely applied, from Iraq to Sri Lanka to the ex-Yugoslavia, but nowhere have its effects been ambiguous to such a degree as they have in Bosnia. What the Yugoslavian conflict really demonstrates is that humanitarian activism is no substitute for political will. Throughout the war in Bosnia, European nations were content to protect relief convoys, never taking any sort of action likely to put an end to the massacres, deportations, or detention camps. The international community, unable to meet its political responsibilities at the outset of the Yugoslavian conflict, put itself in a position where it could do no more than offer humanitarian aid as an appendage to ethnic cleansing, since it later shirked its obligations to asylum seekers under the pretext of not wishing to facilitate this despicable process ... Under cover of European outrage at the Bosnian tragedy, the entire humanitarian movement is now enabling a fresh evasion. Creating security zones and organizing relief convoys cannot become an alibi for refusing to grant asylum to population groups most at risk.

Protecting the Right to Asylum

The ex-Yugoslavia has cast the resigned passivity of European nations in a particularly cold, clear light. It also constitutes a moment of truth for refugee policies because, once again, the victims of war are stranded at Europe's borders. For the first time since the Second World War, Europe finds itself directly facing a mass exodus of refugees: since the outset of the conflict in Croatia and Bosnia more than three million people have been displaced by fighting or ethnic cleansing, and nearly 700,000 refugees have found asylum in other European countries, primarily Germany, Austria, and Hungary. Thought to be limited to the Southern Hemisphere, the problem of war refugees is once again knocking at Europe's door in an atmosphere stamped more than ever by insularity and dread of migrations.

The lack of eagerness on the part of Western nations to welcome, on their soil, civilian populations detained in camps, whose "discovery" in July 1992 had nonetheless inspired outrage amongst the international public—whose liberation, moreover, had been declared an "urgent priority" in August 1992 at the London conference—furnishes evidence for the exceptionally critical issue of the gap that exists between proclaimed values and political skittishness. The liberation, negotiated in September by the International Committee of the Red Cross, of 6,000 detained people packed inside camps in conditions that truly defy the conscience of Europe, had to be delayed because too few host countries came forward. Indeed, it was not until December that the offers of 22 countries could meet the needs of this singularly threatened population. For its part, France—faithful to its reputation as the "land of asylum"—extended offers of temporary asylum to 385 detainees along with their families. But at the beginning of February only 219 of them had actually found refuge in our country, due to the slow acceptance process. Meanwhile, in Croatia and Bosnia two-thirds of the detainees due to be freed continued to face the privation, abuses, and executions that are the common fate in Yugoslavian detention camps …

The reluctance of European nations to offer even temporary asylum to several thousand persons whose survival is directly threatened offers troubling evidence of the insular sentiment currently prevailing in Europe. Conflating refugees and migrants, European nations are trying to deter asylum seekers from knocking at their doors by employing an increasingly restrictive interpretation of the 1951 convention. As a result, the harmonization of refugee policies, a vital step in creating a European space free of internal borders, is evolving in a way detrimental to the right of asylum and the founding values of the European democracies. But in addition to a general toughening of the rules of admission, the Schengen and Dublin Conventions—much like the 1951 convention—continue to ignore the crucial problem of war refugees. In truth, massive, unregulated exoduses of war victims fit awkwardly with European policies for the planned reduction of migrant flows; states are in dread of any unpredictable expansion of their international commitments.

With spreading violence on their borders, the nations of Europe are attempting to fend off asylum seekers. Existing international legal instruments acknowledge the right to seek asylum, but impose no obligation on states to grant that right. At the most, the 1951 convention establishes the principle of non-return of refugees to their own countries "where their lives or their freedom would be at risk." Thus arose the problem, about a decade ago, of "de facto refugees" in Europe—refugees not formally recognized as such, but who nevertheless may not be returned to war-torn countries. The crisis in the ex-Yugoslavia further exposed the ambiguities of European policies, and many countries temporarily suspended the examination of asylum requests for persons native to Bosnia, Serbia, or Croatia. This freeze in proceedings underscores the absence of a formal legal framework to deal with the problem of war refugees within Europe. Generally speaking, the nations of Europe have been content with widely varying, ad hoc responses to the issue of war refugees. Some treat them as legal refugees, others as humanitarian cases. France, for its part, has yet to formulate a policy on the issue of refugees from the ex-Yugoslavia, apart from declining to forcibly return those who have managed, in spite of all obstacles, to reach its territory. The Interior and Social Affairs Ministries have, to be sure, published announcements of visa waivers that authorize three-to-six month stays, renewable. Still, refugees are tolerated for humanitarian reasons alone, living in the most precarious circumstances imaginable, their fate hostage to discretionary decisions by the authorities.

Towards a Policy for War Refugees

The ex-Yugoslavian conflict gives fresh urgency to the task of establishing a legal framework built on European consensus together with an institutional mechanism for responding to the problem of war refugees. The mass flight of war victims towards Europe's borders ought to galvanize legislators and politicians on an issue of vital importance to the European Community's future. The goal, in any case, is not so much to lay the foundations of a new system of protection as it is to harmonize and codify existing practices, and offer relief from insecurity by according legal status to persons who are fleeing violence, seek refuge in Europe, and cannot be returned to their countries.

The question of a legal framework could, in theory, be resolved using existing legal instruments. Indeed, as victims of persecutions "based on …

their religion or their nationality," many Bosnian refugees who were victims of ethnic cleansing perfectly fit the criteria of the 1951 convention. But the mood of insularity currently prevailing in Europe is hardly favorable to an expansive interpretation of the convention and still less to the creation of new legal instruments that might account for populations victimized by violence or new forms of collective persecution. The most realistic solution would be to preserve the 1951 convention as a foundation and supplement it with a regional legal instrument with an expanded definition that would include de facto refugees or war refugees, similar to the OAU convention for Africa or the Cartagena declaration for Latin America.[6]

Simultaneous with this expansion of the definition of refugee, the goal would be to establish procedures for determining refugee status that are consistent with circumstances of mass exodus triggered by conflict situations and widespread disturbances. All generous refugee policies do, in fact, combine an unrestrictive admission policy, based on honoring the right of asylum, with a sorting process that advocates for refugees and migrants. In the current context of identity-based tensions, restrictive immigration policies, and a growing number of population movements, criteria should be found to protect those most at risk. This problem—a highly sensitive one over the past decade due to an ever more restrictive interpretation of the concept of persecution that is contrary to the spirit, if not the letter, of the 1951 convention—is especially critical with respect to war refugees who do not necessarily fit individual criteria and may be clogging proceedings for status determination. The individual-oriented mechanisms established in Europe in the 1950s are truly ill suited to deal with the large-scale migrations generated by conflicts today. Here again, Europeans could draw lessons from experiences in Asia, Africa, and Latin America, where the prima facie procedure affords collective recognition of refugees when mass arrivals do not allow for a case-by-case status determination.

Faced with an increasing number of conflicts at Europe's borders, many countries are thinking of granting temporary status to war refugees on a collective basis. The UNHCR is not opposed to this, provided they are treated

---

[6] Regarding this point, see the recommendations of the European Council on Refugees and Exiles (ECRE), *Working Paper on the Need for a Supplementary Refugee Definition* (Rome, November 1992).

in a manner equal to that of other refugees and consistent with the rights guaranteed by the 1951 convention. Faced with the largest exodus of refugees in Europe since the Second World War, states cannot go on indefinitely dealing with the problem in a provisional fashion—which they characterize as "humanitarian." They have a duty to formulate a clear policy and fulfill their obligations as signatories of the 1951 convention. Their first obligation is to honor the right to asylum. The second is to implement procedures for status determination that are rapid, fair, and suitably adapted to the circumstances of mass migrations. The third obligation is to treat war victims humanely and to guarantee them asylum, assistance, and protection until circumstances have sufficiently improved for them to envision returning, in complete safety, to their country of origin.

CHAPTER FOURTEEN

Humanitarian Action and Politics: A Marriage from Hell

Originally published in *Croissance*, No. 367, January 1994

After the fall of the Berlin Wall the right of intervention was propelled into the foreground. Jeers or applause?

A conversation with Mario Bettati and François Jean

Mario Bettati is Professor of International Law at the Université de Paris II, Panthéon-Assas. Among his writings is *Le Devoir d'Ingérence* [The Duty to Intervene], with Bernard Kouchner, published in 1987 (Editions Denoël). **François Jean** is Head of Mission at Médecins Sans Frontières. He has just edited *Face aux Crises* [Life, Death, and Aid] (Hachette Pluriel), which discusses the increasingly blurred line between humanitarian action and politics.

Mario Bettati, you helped introduce the notion of the right of humanitarian intervention, which has recently come under scathing criticism. Aren't you a bit disappointed in your offspring?

MB: Not at all. People who attack the right of intervention are going after the wrong target. They wrongly confuse what is properly the scope of humanitarian action and what is properly that of politics. Now that the fall of the Berlin Wall has deprived political leaders of any overarching policy doctrine, there is an unfortunate tendency to seek refuge behind a façade of humanitarian action, and too often this becomes a substitute for real diplomatic reflection. Of course I disapprove of this. But I will go on making the case for the right of intervention—because it works. UN member states are looking upon it with increasing favor, and the principle of unimpeded access to victims[1] appears more and more frequently in the texts of resolutions.

---

[1] The legal term corresponding to the media-favored "right of intervention"

François Jean, the right of intervention is, in a sense, what the "French Doctors" have been seeking for 20 years now. You've just published a very disapproving book on the subject. What is your disagreement with the right of intervention?

FJ: We've never claimed any sort of right of intervention for the international community. What we have been adhering to, for 20 years in the field, is a duty to provide care. The right of intervention is a completely different issue. There was a period of euphoria after the fall of the Berlin Wall: the renewed activity at the UN Security Council had convinced us that mass killings under cover of national borders could no longer occur, and that an international system for protecting populations in danger was being established ... Today, in hindsight, the right of intervention appears deeply ambiguous and expedient, because it is so selective. Governments only apply it where there is political advantage, media focus, or public pressure.

MB: I regret that the way the right is being exercised doesn't reflect advances in the law. But just because a law is not implemented doesn't mean it isn't there. It just indicates that current sanctions regimes are flawed.

All the same, would you agree with François Jean that the right of intervention is being implemented in a way that varies according to circumstances?

MB: Yes, of course. But, again, this has nothing to do with humanitarian action. We should point the finger at those who don't apply the principle of unimpeded access to victims often enough—political leaders.

FJ: We aren't criticizing these legal advances. And we're only too happy to see the UN member states recognize a concept of international society that is based not on power relationships alone but also on values, and not just on national sovereignty but on human rights as well ...

Still, you write that in Somalia humanitarian action is being stifled by the military. Why?

FJ: The right of intervention presupposes action by states—which by nature promote their own interests. So, when governments intrude on humanitarian terrain they undermine the fundamental principles that have always allowed nongovernmental organizations (NGOs) to function since the beginning:

independence and impartiality. Also, when it is exercised, the right of intervention creates a dangerous conflation between humanitarian action and politics. We waved the flag of humanitarian action both in Iraq and Somalia so we could intervene militarily. Now, in Somalia, we have the perverse effects of this blurring of roles right before our eyes: it only resulted in reducing the space for humanitarian action, because the Somalis have consistently lumped NGOs together with the UN army that landed under the humanitarian banner. From the moment the Blue Helmets really became a party to the conflict, NGOs have been targeted in the same way as the military by General Aidid's militia and other clans hostile to the intervention. On the whole these developments represent an extraordinary setback, in our view, for the notion established by the International Committee of the Red Cross (ICRC) of a neutral space open solely to independent, impartial organizations. That isn't to say there is no role for governments to play at all, especially on the political and diplomatic levels. It is up to them to exert pressure to end human rights violations and push for negotiated solutions. It is up to them to back up peace accords with military force, as in Cambodia or El Salvador. The international community also needs to be involved financially to enable relief operations for threatened populations. Look how weak the response was to the recent crisis in Burundi that generated 600,000 refugees and tens of thousands of displaced persons! But, first and foremost, NGOs really have to be allowed to intervene as the independent and impartial humanitarian actors they are. Because they are the ones best equipped to gain access to the victims.

So, do we really need a new law? I'm not so sure, especially when I see international forces in Somalia openly flouting the humanitarian law they are supposed to be enforcing, by firing on civilians or the offices of organizations—the AICF, in the present case. Instead of creating a new law that is deeply ambiguous, it would be better to request that states observe existing law—the Geneva Conventions.[2]

---

[2] Completed and revised in 1949, the Geneva Conventions concern the treatment of the wounded, the sick, and prisoners of war as well as govern the protection of civilians during times of war. They specifically prohibit the taking of hostages, summary executions, and torture … Persons protected under the conventions must have access at all times to the assistance of a protecting power (a neutral government charged with safeguarding their interests) as well as the International Committee of the Red Cross. Deportations or population transfers are prohibited.

MB: You criticize military interventions for humanitarian purposes. But who fed Sarajevo? The UN High Commissioner for Refugees did. The NGOs all do a magnificent job, but it's nothing anywhere near what the UN agencies do. And who does the dirty work? The Blue Helmets. Isn't that a form of military action? How can you criticize them? I'm not disparaging what the NGOs do, but why pick a fight with governments that intervene in the humanitarian sphere? There's plenty of room for everyone—unfortunately.

As for the Geneva Conventions: I teach them and I support them. But they're no panacea ... What do the Geneva Conventions cover, anyway? They don't protect the right to live. They regulate how the killing is done. They don't prohibit assaults or injuries; they make rules for how to treat the injured. They represent the minimum required, nothing more. You're outraged that Blue Helmets fired on the AICF's headquarters in Mogadishu. That was unacceptable, of course. But let's keep some perspective. Between the moment the allied troops landed in Normandy in June 1944 and their entry into Berlin in May 1945, didn't a few shells fall on churches, hospitals, or schools?

François Jean, why are you championing these "a-moral" conventions?

FJ: I'm somewhat mystified. Mario Bettati devotes a great deal of energy to promoting the rule of law, yet he doesn't really take the Geneva Conventions very seriously. As imperfect as they are, these minimal rules need to be observed, especially by a UN army intervening for supposedly humanitarian reasons.

MB I absolutely agree. But only if we are clear that this problem is limited to southern Mogadishu. So let's not pass judgment on the entire UN operation in Somalia based on that one instance! In the French sector, where our contingent negotiated the militias' disarmament, everything has gone quite well.

FJ: That's right, the problem is limited to the Somali capital. But I think it's a characteristic example, because blunders of this kind are inherent to any military operation that defines itself solely on a humanitarian basis. We're dealing with a political void in Somalia. The factions haven't been disarmed, and at no time have initiatives been taken to resume the dialogue or to try to begin a process of national reconciliation. Now, if we want crisis management to remain a viable option—if we don't want humanitarian intervention to be written off once and for all—then we need to learn from what happened in Mogadishu.

Mario Bettati, you acknowledge that blurring the line between humanitarian and political-military action is a dangerous thing. How can it be avoided?

MB: The media holds the solution, but it is tyrannized by the ratings. The media and humanitarian representatives both end up distorting the message to contend with an erratic public opinion. Victims' statistics are exaggerated—there is verbal inflation. You can't say "massacre"—you have to say "genocide." It's entertainment-humanitarianism, and we all get caught up in it. Humanitarian action has become a consumer product. "They've touched our hearts, so let's pay ... " We're all individually responsible.

Is that really the basis of the conflation of political-military action and humanitarian action?

MB: Yes, because political authorities are tempted to borrow legitimacy from humanitarian action and turn it to their own ends. You know, it's not political authorities I'm endorsing; it is state-led humanitarian action in cases where I think it's more effective than private-sphere humanitarian action. No NGO can mobilize and deploy Transalls. People often claim that if it hadn't been for state-led humanitarian action, a Western military intervention would already have occurred in Bosnia—even that humanitarian action is responsible for perpetuating the war. It's like saying opening your umbrella makes it rain ... The way things are going, soon they'll be criticizing humanitarian action the same way they used to criticize charity—"charity doesn't equal justice."

FJ: That's right—humanitarian action has become a consumer product like any other; a fashionable notion everyone uses for their own purposes. This is exactly why we need to make a real effort to better define the sphere of humanitarian action. If we don't, it is doomed to become a sort of catchall where political leaders—who are having more and more trouble defining their own foreign policy goals—can offload their responsibilities.

Is it possible, ultimately, for ethics to play a role in international relations?

FJ: I wouldn't offer an opinion on what is or is not ultimately possible. But our role as humanitarian actors is to prod the politicians, to urge them on. And to promote our ideas in such a way that governments will take other dimensions into account besides mere power relationships. But we're not under any illusion. Politics has its own rules—we see ourselves as rebels more than anything else, gadflies. We don't believe in happily ever after.

MB: I think ethics always influences diplomacy and international law. But it operates by a geological clock—very slowly. Adopting the Universal Declaration of Human Rights in Paris on December 10, 1948, didn't spark a movement on December 11 to democratize the planet. The treaties implementing it were passed in 1966; they took effect in 1976, and the Berlin Wall fell in 1989. I think the humanitarian movement, in the end, will change international law. In particular it will supplement the Geneva Conventions, which make humanitarian intervention conditional on a government's consent. The fact that the United Nations keeps reiterating the principle of unimpeded access to victims in resolution after resolution will allow us to do without a government's approval if need be.

So, on the whole, a sort of worldwide awareness is emerging?

MB: Ten years ago no one was talking about humanitarian action at the United Nations—neither in the General Assembly nor in the cafeteria … Now it's all they do talk about. The success of the ethical values of humanitarian organizations has made everyone realize that the international community can impose minimum standards and that certain things will not be tolerated. Still, just because we're sending in ambulances doesn't mean we can fail to point out the real political dilemmas in Bosnia or that we can afford to botch the analysis of the situation in southern Mogadishu. Solid gains have been made: today no government opposes the principle of unimpeded access for medical convoys. Which is not the same thing as unimpeded access for armored divisions, I agree. Some 60-odd Security Council resolutions reiterate that principle.

FJ: It's clear a worldwide awareness has emerged over the past several years, rooted in a new perception of problems around the world and a consensus on what is unacceptable. But there have never been so many atrocities committed as there have since this new trend of humanitarian law began. Because there's a contradiction between, on the one hand, real advances happening at the level of international institutions and, on the other, the weakening of the nation-state. Yes, more and more resolutions are passed, but they have hardly any effect on the ground. Legal frameworks collapse and armed groups splinter and divide—in order to enforce the law you still need responsible interlocutors who can be held to the commitments they've made. Well, they are getting harder and harder to find.

MB: I'm not denying the reality of facts on the ground. But that in no way condemns every effort at formulating laws and standards. The rise of Stalinism and Maoism and all the third-world dictatorships occurred in the years following the adoption of the Universal Declaration of Human Rights. So that means we shouldn't have adopted the Universal Declaration of Human Rights?

FJ: I have the feeling that NGOs have always been willing to infringe upon the law. Which is not to say they disregard it: it helps hold some of the interlocutors to their commitments. But we're helpless against armed gangs. The repressive state is fading away, but at the same time so is the state's ability to govern.

MB: That's the main thing. For a long time we thought the major threat to human rights was a too-strong state. But there's another threat out there: the absence of the state.

Interviewer: Sandrine Tolotti

Chapter Fifteen

Compromised Humanitarian Action?

Originally published in *Panoramiques*, No.15, spring 1994, p.123-129

Nils Andersson: Two Security Council resolutions have introduced a new concept—the right of humanitarian intervention. Security Council Resolution 688, adopted April 5, 1991, allowed humanitarian teams to enter Iraq to provide relief aid to Kurdish groups, and 794, adopted December 3, 1992, requested that "all necessary means"—including military—be utilized to allow relief operations to proceed in Somalia. The duty to provide humanitarian assistance is undisputed. Should the right of humanitarian intervention be viewed the same way?

Francois Jean: Personally, I'm not so sure these two resolutions confirm the emergence of a "right to humanitarian intervention," because it seems to me this right is being exercised in a highly expedient manner, totally contingent on individual circumstances. On the other hand, these two resolutions clearly mark a real departure on two levels. First of all, they expand the United Nations' system of collective security to include internal crises—until now the system had only been applied in cases of international conflict. They also cleared the way for interventions of the type defined in Chapter VII of The UN charter, which authorizes the use of force in the event of a threat to international peace and security. For the first time, really, a link has been established between events occurring within the borders of a nation-state, in cases of massive human rights violations, and international peace and security. Resolution 688 on Iraq establishes this link based on the danger of influxes of refugees over international borders, and Resolution 794 on Somalia characterized the Somali tragedy itself as a threat to peace and security. Also, and this is the second major feature of these resolutions, it is striking that in both cases humanitarian concerns have been singled out as justifying international intervention to deal with a repressive regime or a failed nation-state. Resolution 688 expressly stipulates that humanitarian organizations be granted immediate access to victims of repression, and Resolution 794 authorizes international forces to utilize all necessary means to establish secure conditions for humanitarian relief operations. In Iraq, just as in Somalia, humanitarianism is the key argument for intervention. This fact brings two thoughts to mind—one fairly optimistic, the other somewhat skeptical.

It seems to me that this emergence of humanitarian concerns as a justification for and a goal of intervention by the international community is a result of deep, underlying changes in the international scene. The collapse of totalitarianism marked the triumph of liberal democracy, the only political system which treats people as ends in themselves. The human rights "revolution" at the end of the 1980s reflected the emergence of a new global awareness based on a new sense of the problems the world faces and a new consensus concerning the limits of what is acceptable. National sovereignty is still the norm, but it can sometimes be contested by virtue of fresh aspirations that place human dignity at the heart of international politics. This concept of international order, centered more on values than on power relationships and more on people than on nations, is gathering momentum despite hesitation in diplomatic circles.

Having said all that, and this is my second comment, it doesn't necessarily follow that intervention has become the rule and that it will no longer be possible to slaughter on a massive scale under cover of one's own borders. Behind the idea—which the notion of an international community legitimizes—of a harmonious world consensus based on humanist values, nation-states still act according to self-interests and defend their sovereignty tooth and nail. It would be mistaken in theory and unwise in practice to imagine that Resolutions 688 and 794 will amount to the first draft of a new system for protecting population groups in their own countries. Mistaken in theory, because nations intervene not as part of some campaign for universal solidarity but out of a sense of their own self-interest. Unwise in practice, because any international intervention, if it is to be credible, presupposes a degree of political will that is unlikely except in extraordinary circumstances. In Iraq in 1991 it took a sense of responsibility on the part of the West along with an entire nation running amok on TV and overrunning the borders of neighboring countries to provoke an international response. But most of all it required a demonstrable self-interest on the part of Western countries. The international intervention was not so much a case of spontaneous involvement as it was the completion of a service contract, in extremis. Its purpose was to preserve the appearance of a just war and avert a fresh refugee problem by encouraging threatened Kurds to return home with the offer of protection—only too temporary—in northern Iraq.

Similarly, the "humanitarian intervention" in the ex-Yugoslavia served essentially as an alibi to camouflage the West's acceptance of aggression and create the impression of international engagement ... Politicians have always been tempted to clothe themselves in the mantle of morality, to disguise their interests—or indifference—behind a seamless façade of good intentions. The current outpouring of speeches on intervention—or rather the recent outpouring, since it has barely been mentioned for several months now—is little more than a new instance of this old temptation. In short, of course we're more than happy with emerging demands for solidarity in our own societies. But let's not be under any illusion; TV-conditioned emotions are quite often fleeting. And we should make no mistake; this celebrated right of intervention is going to remain expedient and selective—contingent on political interest, media exposure, and the pressure of public opinion.

NA: According to an interview with Rony Brauman, president of Médecins Sans Frontières, the toolbox of international law includes several provisions on the protection of civilians in time of war. Unlike ad hoc resolutions, these provisions have a binding effect on those governments that have ratified them. So one of the effects of these recent resolutions is to weaken humanitarian law instead of reinforcing it.

FJ: That's obviously an important underlying question, given this spreading notion that from now on the international community will be resolved never again to tolerate massive human rights violations. What legal instruments are available? Basically the UN charter and the Geneva Conventions. The UN charter is, to say the least, ill suited to deal with present-day issues: it refers only to international conflicts and wars of aggression waged by conventional armies. It makes no mention of the internal crises and civil wars that constitute most of today's conflicts. But in practice there have been developments on the ground that have had the effect of eroding the principle of sovereignty we were just speaking of, permitting UN interventions in internal crises under certain circumstances. Then there are the Geneva Conventions and the additional 1977 protocols concerning non-international conflicts. Do we need to develop new legal instruments? Personally, I don't think so. To me, the Geneva Conventions seem quite well suited to present-day crises; they deal fully with our own concerns regarding the protection of civilians and noncombatants and respect for humanitarian workers. The problem is that too often the conventions are not applied, even though the signatories are committed to "observing and enforcing the observation" of the core principles of international human rights law. So the goal, in my opinion, is not to develop new legal instruments but to strengthen existing law by enforcing it, in a manner consistent with what the signatory governments themselves have committed to.

Unfortunately that's not happening, and one gets the impression that the Geneva conventions are increasingly being ignored by the very parties meant to be enforcing them. Unfortunately, if a law isn't used, it gradually falls into abeyance. The conventions are in no way strengthened by all the resolutions now being passed—these seem more like ad hoc gestures meant to convey the impression of responsiveness and commitment. Montesquieu said, "Useless laws make necessary laws weaker," and unfortunately this idea very much applies to the current situation. Bosnia is a good illustration of a crisis where the core principles of humanitarian law are trampled underfoot every day, in spite of a deluge of Security Council resolutions. Throughout the war in Bosnia, Western countries never made the slightest move to halt the massacres, deportations, or internment of civilians in camps. The West remained passive until August 1992, when the camps were discovered and the public outcry forced them to react. But repeated resolutions had no effect, and the belated creation, in May 1993, of the first international war crimes tribunal since Nuremburg in no way alters the situation: nothing is being done to halt the abuses against civilians, and the absence of funding leaves the impression that this is essentially a cosmetic measure.

Not only do ad hoc resolutions that authorize international intervention to deliver aid to victims fail to strengthen existing legal instruments—they can also be fraught with consequences for compliance with humanitarian law. In Bosnia and Somalia, for example, international forces—not content

117

with failing to enforce the Geneva Conventions—openly flout them. In fact, in both cases, the Security Council resolutions are restricted to the protection of convoys and relief teams; they are silent regarding the protection of victims. Far worse, the Blue Helmets' conduct frequently runs counter to the core principles of humanitarian law. In Bosnia, for example, the United Nations negotiated prisoner exchanges—although the Geneva Conventions affirm the principle of unilateral, unconditional prisoner releases. As a result the International Committee of the Red Cross (ICRC) was reduced to impotence, since there was always a better deal to be had from one "humanitarian" actor or another ... The situation is even more serious in Somalia, where international forces openly trample on the Geneva Conventions. UNOSOM Blue Helmets seem to be above the law: they enjoy total impunity and apparently place no limits on the use of force. So they have not hesitated to attack hospitals or the offices of humanitarian organizations, in flagrant violation of Geneva Convention provisions. Similarly, the excessive use of force has created hundreds of civilian victims since the intervention began—although humanitarian law expressly provides for the protection of civilian populations in conflict zones.

NA: It would be interesting to discuss the impact, positive or perverse, on the respective countries and peoples involved when the right of humanitarian intervention has been asserted, as in Iraq, Somalia, or the ex-Yugoslavia—or where the United Nations and the international community remained more or less silent, as in Burma, Sudan, or Georgia.

FJ: You raise two basic issues there: one is nonintervention, and the other is the impact of intervention when the international community does decide to become involved in internal conflicts. The decision not to intervene goes to the issue of selectivity we were speaking about earlier. This is the point of view that says we need to be able to distinguish the forest from the trees; Iraq and Somalia remain the exception, and many crises involving massive abuses arouse no reaction whatsoever. The tragedies in Sudan, Burma, or Afghanistan, for example, meet with nothing but indifference on the part of the international community. For our own part, we try as much as we can to keep these forgotten tragedies from being buried in obscurity—unfortunately without much success. For example, for a year and a half we tried in vain to draw the attention of the international community to the tragedy unfolding in Somalia. It took until 1992 for Western countries to finally focus on that shattered country which, in the meantime, had plunged into severe famine. Clearly, with tragedies of this magnitude, the international community's involvement is indispensable in meeting the needs of threatened population groups.

Still, this doesn't mean we believe military intervention is a desirable thing, because an intervention of that kind poses enormous problems. The first problem is the difficulty of intervening in internal crises, magnified by the fact that the United Nations is still ill prepared for this kind of intervention. As you know, throughout the Cold War, the United Nations intervened only in the context of what is called peacekeeping, the basic principles of which are the consent of the warring parties and the nonuse of force. The need now is to go beyond these parameters, which were perfectly suited to the zero-sum game of the Cold War but no longer correspond to what is required for interventions in civil wars. These interventions are not at all straightforward; they raise a number of issues. We could start off by asking ourselves to what extent outsiders can provide solutions to internal conflicts if the warring parties themselves aren't ready to seek a negotiated way out. But apart from that underlying issue, these interventions pose two types of problems.

The first problem concerns the United Nations' capacities for intervention in internal conflicts. Intervening without the acquiescence of parties during a full-blown crisis is obviously of a totally different nature than deploying Blue Helmets between warring parties that have agreed to suspend hostilities. At a time when there are more and more interventions under the authority of Chapter VII, the United Nations needs to adapt itself to the new rules of the game. The operations launched recently in Bosnia and Somalia did, in fact, reveal serious flaws in terms of how mandates are defined, the rules of engagement, the chain of command, and coordination between the various contingents.

In addition to those military aspects, it is also clearly essential that we improve coordination between the different elements of the UN system. This issue, which unfortunately is not a new one in an organization with a great many specialized agencies that enjoy extensive autonomy, and often operate virtually like fiefdoms, is an especially urgent one for the ever larger and more complex operations currently being mounted. Further, the United Nations needs to build up its operational capacities in order to intervene effectively in emergency situations. At a moment when "emergency" seems to have become the new watchword, UN agencies must adapt themselves to contexts in which there are often no government interlocutors and which involve extreme danger and chaotic developments on the ground. These current crises represent a true challenge for the United Nations; it needs to be more flexible and adaptable in order to respond to the needs of population groups in crisis zones.

The second problem goes to the difficulty of coupling humanitarian with military-oriented approaches in operations that blend peacekeeping and emergency relief. Somalia has thrown a particularly harsh light on the perverse impact such interventions can have. While the initial objective was to establish secure conditions for humanitarian relief operations, the international intervention actually exacerbated tensions and made it more dangerous for humanitarian workers. By limiting themselves to the logic of war making alone, the Blue Helmets became one of the participants in the conflict, undermining the principles of neutrality and impartiality that are key to creating an atmosphere of trust with warring parties and preserving access to the victims. The military escalation in Mogadishu is fraught with consequences for future efforts to conduct relief operations. Humanitarian organizations—now associated in the minds of local residents with a military force that represents itself humanitarian—are the victims of this confusion, and their opportunities for action are sharply curtailed.

Unfortunately Somalia is not the only instance in which the blurring of the humanitarian and the political has reduced humanitarian space. This issue is of major concern to us; it underscores how urgent it is for us to reflect upon our principles, in a time when the humanitarian field is ever more crowded with new actors.

NA: In cases where the United Nations and the international community do not intervene, does that handicap your ability to deliver aid—and, on the other hand, when there is humanitarian intervention by the international community, does that increase the resources available to you?

FJ: In spite of the problems and the perverse impacts I just mentioned, we need the international community and the United Nations. Not for our protection—more often than not the results of such protection are mixed or even counterproductive—but to respond to the needs of population groups. Alone, organizations like MSF quite clearly do not have the capacity to deal with very large-scale crises. In situations like Somalia last year or, for a number of years, Sudan, the needs are so great that it calls for resources well beyond those available to nongovernmental organizations (NGOs). If you take Somalia, for example, we tried to respond to the food crisis, which was acute even in early 1992, by establishing therapeutic feeding centers. But setting up centers like these makes no sense unless an overall system of food distribution is operating at the same time, and we didn't have the capacity to launch an operation of that scale. Fortunately the ICRC was able to mount an enormous food aid operation, but despite all its efforts it couldn't meet the entire range of needs, given the climate of insecurity that prevailed. In the United Nations' absence, the few organizations present in Somalia at the beginning of 1992 had to try to cope by launching aid programs disproportionate to their means. Clearly, the involvement of UN agencies was vital at that point. They alone had the resources to head off the rush towards the precipice, and their absence had serious consequences for the affected population groups, as the secretary-general's representative Mohamed Sahnoun made clear.

This is the issue. It's not about our programs, which we always have the resources to implement. But in acute crises these programs make no sense unless they are part of the kind of large-scale relief operations that, given the dimensions of the needs, only the UN system can conduct. It is clear NGOs and the UN agencies are genuinely complementary. The problem in Somalia is that this complementariness couldn't come into play until the fall of 1992, though by then it was already too late, and the country had been beset by famine for six months. Fortunately, this situation isn't the norm, and in many cases the combined efforts of humanitarian organizations and UN agencies make it possible to avert disasters.

On the whole we have good relations with the UN agencies, be it with the High Commissioner for Refugees, with whom we have a special relationship, UNICEF, or the World Food Program. Naturally these relationships vary depending on the personalities of officials on the ground and the operational capacities of the different agencies.

NA: Where NGOs intervene they need to understand the territory, the people, the mentalities, habits, traditions, customs, etc. In countries where the United Nations has exercised the right of humanitarian intervention, do its workers always take sufficient care not to "damage the self-respect of the peoples" they are helping or aiding?

FJ: At times some of the very sizeable operations tend to deploy like enormous machines, crushing everything in their path. Again, Somalia is a caricatured example of the lack of respect some workers have for the societies where they've been brought to work. Some statements early in the intervention conveyed the image of a country that was a kind of no-man's-land roamed by bloodthirsty, drug-addicted hooligans. I'm not denying that Somali society had been profoundly de-structured by war and famine or that the violence had reached levels seldom equaled—but to go from that to such a caricatured depiction … this profound ignorance of Somali society and utter incomprehension of the dynamics of the crisis probably had a lot to do with the escalation of violence later on—as if merely killing a gang of delinquents could be the solution to an upheaval of this magnitude …

I shouldn't generalize, but it really must be admitted that the personnel, both military and civilian, of international operations are not always respectful of the peoples and local traditions, as the behavior of certain contingents of Blue Helmets in Cambodia showed. For our own part we are quite sensitive to this issue, for two reasons. The first has to do with what "makes us tick"—a humanitarian commitment that is fundamentally connected to concern for others and respect for human dignity. It's inconceivable to us to see a victim we are delivering aid to as no more than a digestive apparatus. The people we deal with are people we want to work with and have a give-and-take with. In times of acute crisis we want to help people reestablish their capacities for choice. We don't see them simply as people getting handouts—nor would we presume to work out for them what their goals should be as a society. The second reason goes to the need to understand, in order to act. We do not intervene inside some philanthropic bubble but in complex societies that have histories and are dense with conflicts and power relationships. If you are going to be able to assist the victims in these crisis zones, where aid is usually a resource to be battled over by the warring parties, it is vital to have a good understanding of the dynamics of the crisis and the strategies of the different actors in order to prevent the aid from being diverted from its intended targets.

Having said that, I don't believe NGOs have a monopoly on this sense of solidarity or this understanding of societies. Many UN officials share the same concern for the societies in which they work. The problem is that the cumbersome naature of the process, the weight of the bureaucracy, and the focus on governments as interlocutors sometimes cuts UN personnel off from the realities on the ground. And the hasty recruitment—especially in very large-scale operations—of poorly trained personnel, more focused on their "per diem" than on the fate of the populations they are supposed to be helping, often results in indifferent or contemptuous behavior.

NA: So, there's always the ability to intervene when the United Nations doesn't do so directly, but in particularly severe circumstances, UN intervention becomes necessary and indispensable. This brings to mind something that could be said of the UN machine as a whole: there is much to be criticized, but nonetheless it remains indispensable. So it's not a question of writing the United Nations off, but gaining more insight and considering how to enhance its role and mission. In the charter's preamble it says, "We the peoples"—in reality the peoples are absent, for the most part. Do you think NGOs are, or can be, one vehicle of communication for "We the peoples"—a moral force in the UN machine—precisely where diplomacy, cynicism, and state-to-state politics are most dominant?

FJ: I do think that NGOs, in a sense, mirror the independence and efforts of their own societies; they also embody a demand for solidarity that is surfacing in many societies now, projecting it across national borders by bringing individuals or groups from different cultures and backgrounds together in common projects. There has been a lot of discussion about the phenomenon of globalization in the spheres of economics, finance, and the media. This phenomenon is just as apparent in the field of international relations. It is manifested in the appearance of new actors and the building of new networks that play an increasingly important role parallel to the traditional, state-to-state channels. The growing role of NGOs is one of the best examples of these changes. It is an indication of the gradual erosion of the nation-state, long considered the lone actor on the international scene. At the time the United Nations was created, immediately after the war, the nation-state was the fulcrum of the international scene. The centrality of the state was later reaffirmed—and virtually worshipped—during the period of decolonization. This was perfectly understandable in a period marked by the emergence of new nation-states eager for recognition, aspiring to take their place on the international stage. But the international scene has undergone profound transformation since then, and the United Nations is still to a great extent stuck in traditional patterns. It needs to evolve and reshape itself to a new reality that no longer turns on state-to-state relations alone.

True, UN authorities too often tend only to deal with government interlocutors and are too accommodating to existing regimes on the assumption that it isn't their role to take on member states. It's time for the United Nations to evolve, to reckon with the new aspirations the public is expressing, and to work closely with the new actors now coming onto the international scene. The United Nations is an indispensable organization: it's an irreplaceable forum for public discussion. In a time when international interventions in crisis zones are more and more numerous, it is a source of authority in crisis management and of legitimacy for those interventions. Likewise, in the area of aid, the United Nations has an essential role to play due to the very substantial financial and operational … resources at its disposal. So it's not a matter of questioning the United Nations' usefulness. But it is nevertheless vital that it adapt itself to current developments, that it rid itself of inflexibility, and that it be more responsive to what societies are saying. From that perspective I believe NGOs need to prod the United Nations and motivate it in the direction of greater openness. And it is up to us to urge the United Nations to reflect upon its own principles, at a time when humanitarian action finds itself increasingly compromised by new actors with claims to intervene in crisis zones.

Chapter Sixteen

From State-to-State to Transnational: The Role of Non-State Actors in Conflicts (The Case of International Humanitarian Organizations)

Originally published in *Recherches et Documents*, No. 5, June 1998

Conflicts in the Aftermath of the Cold War

The analysis of conflicts today has been liberated from the heavy ideological shackles of the Cold War. For a period of 30 years, so-called "low-intensity" conflicts were indeed interpreted through an analytical grid that recast them as marginal manifestations of the confrontation between East and West. Today's conflicts are no longer perceived simply as more or less exotic replicas of the dominant Soviet-American encounter. They can be seen for what they really are: conflicts in which the dynamic of violence is, by and large, locally determined. Obviously, external factors were long overestimated—particularly the East-West dimension; by now the complexity and diversity of conflicts must be readily apparent to all. But it would be regrettable if, in reaction, these conflicts were now perceived as isolated phenomena, irreducible and disconnected from international dynamics. The issue that is truly before us today is how to revitalize conflict analysis.

If the current dominant narrative is to be believed, conflicts have become more numerous in recent years, bloodier, more anarchic, more irrational … Some observers, for lack of any broader explanation, are inclined to replace the old "ideological" reading with an "ethnic" one based on a concept of atavistic violence. Others have rushed to fabricate a new monolithic framework out of this uncertainty: the violence—which they believe has become an uncontrollable global phenomenon—is now a generally diffused peril, they say, ever changing yet ever the same.

The terms "criminalized guerilla fighter" and "transnational mafia" are attempts to lend coherence and unity to this menace supposedly approaching from the Southern Hemisphere.

Naturally, such reclassifications invite deep skepticism. Analysts have neatly demolished the ideological construct of a global peril adopted by certain global security professionals after the end of the East-West confrontation.[1] The chaos-and-barbarity narrative deserves skeptical treatment as well. In contrast to widely held belief, the number of conflicts has not appreciably increased since the end of the Cold War.[2] Likewise, there is nothing to support the notion that contemporary conflicts are now bloodier than was previously the case. To be sure, the Rwandan genocide and the ethnic cleansing in Bosnia exacted a heavy human toll, but it was not an unprecedented one, as attested by the genocide in Cambodia and the civil war in Uganda during the 1970s. This impression of barbarity is no doubt partly rooted in a heightened sensitivity to the question of human rights. Conflicts, no longer interpreted through the prism of East-West confrontation, appear to have lost all meaning and are now seen mainly from the perspective of their human consequences. There is an impression of irrationality that stems from focusing solely on the overall impact conflict has at the societal level—the economic, human, etc., dimensions—while neglecting to analyze the entirely rational interests, goals, and strategies of groups involved in the dynamic of violence.[3]

But it is not the fashionable narrative of the moment that must be reexamined and challenged—rather it is the conventional frames of reference we use for analyzing conflict. The intellectual framework of neorealism—with its primary emphasis on the centrality of the state, a binary system of confrontation, and rigid distinctions between internal and external—seems powerless to explain contemporary forms of conflict. In many cases the weakening of the state leads to a diffusion of violence and new linkages between state and non-state actors, who in turn, some believe,

---

[1] Didier Bigo, "Grands Débats Pour un Petit Monde" [Big Debates for a Small World], *Cultures et Conflits*, no. 19/20 (winter, 1995).

[2] R. Williamson, "The Contemporary Face of Conflict," Annual 1995, *Jane's Intelligence Review*.

[3] David Keen, "A Rational Kind of Madness," *Oxford Development Studies*, vol. 25, no. 1 (February 1997).

reproduce certain of the state's characteristics. Likewise, analyses in terms of the differing force capacities of adversaries on a given piece of territory are becoming less and less relevant. This dualistic emphasis, partly based on the ideological alignments of the warring parties, but mainly on their sources of foreign support in the binary, Cold War context of a super-power confrontation, no longer corresponds to the more splintered, fluid, volatile conflicts of today. The tendency of armed movements to fragment, the increasing number of entrepreneurs of violence, and the formation of networks that to a large degree extend far beyond the borders of conflictual spaces—all of these are generating highly diverse forms of cooperation or confrontation that no longer strictly conform to the traditional model of confrontation between a state and an armed opposition movement. Finally, as the concept of sovereignty fades and networks that defy borders and territories grow stronger, new transactions among local and international actors become possible. The process of globalization, for the most part fully achieved in the economic and financial spheres, now embraces communications, migration, humanitarian aid, environmental protection and waste disposal, criminality and security, violence and diplomacy, and more.

These developments are not unique to conflict situations; they point to the emergence of a new reality that is global yet at the same time fragmented. Today, states are at a loss to deal with overwhelming developments that challenge them at their core: they are unprepared for the profusion of identity-based demands or for internal disturbances and civil wars that are undermining existing political frameworks. They are helpless, as well, to cope with a set of new migration streams spreading across the globe and skirting traditional forms of regulation. War is not a hiatus in the "development process";[4] nor is it a radical departure in the process of globalization. It is an outgrowth, under varying circumstances, of strategies of mobilization and confrontation that, however out of step they may be with the market-democracy model, are nonetheless open to interaction with the outside world. In many cases the political economy of a war is not so different from that of the

---

[4] Mark Duffield, "Complex Emergencies and the Crisis of Developmentalism," in Linking Relief and Development, *IDS Bulletin*, vol. 25, no. 4 (October 1994).

regime it threatens to topple. In African countries dependent on exports of a small number of raw materials, war merely recycles—sometimes even reinforces—time-honored practices by which these resources are appropriated for private use by a few political actors with connections to international middlemen in the parallel economy. Moreover, in certain cases such as Burundi (ivory and gold) and certainly Sierra Leone (diamonds), the causes of war are rooted in overheated competition between different networks struggling within the state to appropriate these export revenues.[5]

But to an increasing extent the state is not needed for purposes of appropriating a country's wealth. During the peak years of "Greater Liberia," Charles Taylor established a form of political rule that eclipsed the national structure and linked up directly with the world market. Liberia offers a good illustration of the transition from a neo-patrimonial approach, focused on conquering the state and seizing the whole national "pie," to that of a trading-post economy based on transactions with foreign companies.[6] This has nothing to do with theories about states supposedly slipping from reliance on their own resources back into dependence on foreign companies and international aid. The conquest of power and its perquisites is always a key goal for most rebel leaders, and, generally speaking, any situation will remain deeply unstable as long as this issue remains unresolved. Nevertheless, new decentralized modes of cooperation with international non-state actors are enabling some armed movements to accumulate power and gain access to the world market. In the case of Liberia, the NPFL [National Patriotic Front of Liberia] earned as much as $400 to $500 million at the start of the 1990s from the extraction of natural resources (iron, wood, rubber, etc.) with the aid of foreign companies. Likewise, in Angola, the resources UNITA [National Union for Total Independence of Angola] obtained between 1992 and 1996 from mining and selling diamonds have been valued at $1.5 billion. And in Zaire, foreign companies, particularly American (American Mineral

---

[5] William Reno, *Corruption and State Politics in Sierra Leone* (Cambridge University Press, 1995).

[6] William Reno, "Reinvention of an African Patrimonial State: Charles Taylor's Liberia," *Third World Quarterly*, vol. 16, no. 1 (1995). See also "War, Markets and the Reconfiguration of West Africa's Weak States," *Comparative Politics* (July 1997); "African Weak States and Commercial Alliances," *African Affairs*, no. 96 (1997).

Fields, etc.), did not wait for the fall of Kinshasa to sign operating agreements with Kabila, the rebel leader.

These developments highlight the importance of transactions between local and international non-state actors in a crisis context, where the state is weak. Far from a hiatus or a fleeting anomaly in a linear process of development, war may instead be a form of response to the problem of globalization and the state. It may contribute, as Charles Tilly would argue, to the process of nation building or to the weakening of the state instead. It might also be one of the ways access is opened up to transnational networks. In any case, it points to the emergence and consolidation of new economic processes as well as new political and societal actors. Among the latter, non-state actors are playing an ever increasing role: political-military movements, military-economic entrepreneurs, "informal" traders, multinational companies, nongovernmental organizations, the media, etc. It is important, therefore, to try to better understand their strategies, their interactions with the state and with civilian populations, their role in the dynamic of violence, and, most important, in terms of transactions and dynamics of cooperation now materializing between actors on the local and international levels.

How linkages grow between the local and international spheres is a seldom-studied area where non-state actors play a significant role. Even excluding the many types of international networks—criminal rings (arms, drugs …), support networks, diasporas, etc., which armed movements establish or exploit to mobilize foreign backing and resources, the international actors ever more numerous in crisis zones are having a rising impact on the dynamics of conflicts in so-called Southern countries. In terms of economics, generally speaking, there are two main forms of linkages with the international sphere: business and aid. In both cases the state's role is beginning to diminish in favor of private actors. With respect to business, the importance of international companies has long been acknowledged; in some countries they now even assume executive functions such as security. As for aid, the last 10 years have been marked by rapid, profound change in the international system of cooperation established at the end of the Second World War as well as during the period of decolonization.

The object of this paper is to study these developments, so keenly impacted by the waning role of the state and the expansion of private international networks, and to analyze their impact on conflicts that are no longer state-to-state, nor even truly intrastate. For this purpose I will focus on humanitarian aid, which in the course of the last decade has become the principal form of international involvement in conflict situations—in any event those that represent no major strategic interest for the major powers (Africa, Afghanistan, Sri Lanka, etc.). First, I will describe how modes of international intervention in countries at war have been transformed. Then I will examine the processes of subcontracting aid and security now at work in crisis situations. Finally, I will attempt to analyze the impact the increased presence of international non-state actors in conflict-ridden countries is having on the dynamics of violence. Does this presence contribute to the weakening of states, political fragmentation, and the proliferation of entrepreneurs of violence? Does it favor the formation of networks that extend beyond spaces of conflict? Does it encourage the supplanting of traditional, state-to-state circuits by new, private transnational networks?

Political Support for Humanitarian Aid

Modes of international intervention in internal conflicts have significantly changed in the past 10 years. Until the end of the 1980s, the superpowers were politically involved in "peripheral" conflicts, providing major support in the form of arms and financing to states or armed opposition movements. The end of the Cold War triggered a drastic reduction in international support for the protagonists of conflicts. With the passing of East-West confrontation, the superpowers largely turned their backs on internal conflicts, which no longer had any clear international importance. Gone are the days when the United States or the Soviet Union supported either the state or the armed opposition in conflicts generally perceived as far-off manifestations of the Cold War. External support, where it continues, comes, for the most part, either from regional powers or those that have taken their place, as in Afghanistan or the ex-Zaire. Even in "strategic zones," Western initiatives are mostly political or diplomatic in nature and represent no significant commitment, as illustrated by the United States' comparatively rapid recovery from its failure in Iraqi Kurdistan or the general reticence in responding to the turmoil in the ex-Yugoslavia and the deteriorating situation in Algeria—regions nonetheless considered crucial for western European security. This is all the more true for regions more distant, where benign neglect seems to be the rule.

But, while the former *padrones* no longer support their "clients," Western nations remain involved in conflict situations, if only as providers of relief aid. Even excluding "military-humanitarian" interventions, there has been a growing tendency for states to intervene on a humanitarian level, especially in crises now devoid of strategic interest. Emergency relief has now taken the place of both political support (typical of the Cold War) and development aid (now largely out of fashion). There has been an appreciable increase in the share of "humanitarian aid" and "emergency aid," as a part of overall Official Development Assistance (ODA), which has decreased in net terms since the end of the 1980s. According to the Development Assistance Committee (DAC) of the Organisation for Economic Co-operation and Development (OECD), the share of "emergency assistance" (not including emergency food aid) went from 1.35 percent to 5.75 percent of ODA between 1980 and 1993.[7] In the European Union (ECHO), as well, there was a 6.6-fold increase in emergency humanitarian aid between 1990 and 1994, from about 120 to more than 760 million ECUs. Since 1994, funding for humanitarian aid seems to have leveled off, and the aid market is starting to expand into another area: conflict prevention and resolution. Donors, seeking cheaper, more rapid solutions to conflicts, have increased their support for organizations engaged in "parallel" diplomacy. But funding for such initiatives is still in its early days, and in many cases humanitarian aid remains the major external resource still injected into conflict situations. Since the start of the 1990s, humanitarian aid has been the West's response of choice to political crises in so-called Southern Hemisphere countries.

State involvement in the humanitarian sphere has been concurrent with the end of East-West confrontation. The collapse of totalitarianism has ushered in the triumph of a form of humanitarianism produced by the illusion—which the notion of an "international community" legitimizes—of all

---

[7] The trend is similar for bilateral aid; the portion dedicated to emergency aid went from 1.5 percent to 8.27 percent between 1982–83 and 1993. In 1993 the emergency aid portion of ODA was 12.18% for Germany, 17% for Holland, 12.38% for Great Britain, and 9.55% for the United States.

humanity finally reuninted in a fresh consensus on what will and will not be tolerated. This humanitarianism is a symptom of disarray in the presence of what is perceived to be a "new international disorder." It is nurtured by the pervasiveness of television, which favors an instant, emotional, and ahistorical response to reality. And it demonstrates that governments in democracies cannot remain deaf to demands from their own societies for solidarity during crises covered by the media. Western engagement is the outcome of a wide variety of motives ranging from humanitarian concerns to political considerations: among these are "image-building strategies" and a desire to manipulate humanitarian action for political purposes. Decisions to intervene emerge from an increasingly complex process that is as much symbolic and financial as it is strictly political and is determined, in the end, by interactions among the media, public opinion, political rulers, and nongovernmental and intergovernmental organizations in the democracies. States are still the major financial donors and as such retain a central role in relief operations, but they are not always pivotal players in a sphere that does not systematically reflect political considerations. In the past few years humanitarian aid has, to be sure, become a significant instrument in the foreign policies of Western nations. But many interventions are only remotely connected to strategies for extending influence or defending national interests—or even to coherent aid policies. Generally speaking, we have gone from state support—direct or indirect, covert or acknowledged—of states or guerilla movements, to humanitarian aid that at times is undertaken with no specific policy objective and is increasingly being delivered through non-state intermediaries with no political agenda of their own.

As humanitarian aid has evolved, the aid system itself has undergone a profound reorganization, as demonstrated by the increasing power of non-state actors and the radical transformation in how emergency aid is implemented, as it reaches inward from the periphery to the centers of conflicts.

The Increasing Power of Non-State Actors

The early 1990s saw a shift away from development aid, in large part granted within the framework of state-to-state relations, towards humanitarian aid increasingly delivered by private actors — i.e. nongovern mental organizations (NGOs).[8]

There has been a fundamental reorganization of actors in the sphere of emergency aid over the past 10 years: despite the emergence of state humanitarianism, national entities play little more than a secondary role in implementing relief operations, apart from "military-humanitarian" interventions; the field is dominated by multilateral organizations and, still more, by increasingly powerful private actors. The role of NGOs in delivering international aid has evolved considerably over the past 10 years. Apart from their own, often considerable private funds raised among the general public, they are also channeling an increasing share of government funding from donor nations.[9] According to the OECD, NGOs raised roughly $8.3 million in 1992, the second largest source of financing for ODA in net terms—behind bilateral aid but a good deal more than the UN system.[10] The trend is especially conspicuous in crisis situations: according to ECHO, from 1990 to 1994 between 45 and 67 percent of funding for emergency aid came from NGOs.

In beneficiary countries, these changes appear to be jeopardizing the state's role as the exclusive channel of access to resources from abroad. Traditionally, the state was the prime beneficiary of international aid. This was especially true for bilateral and multilateral development aid, which was, and essentially still is, managed by beneficiary-state authorities, with

[8] John Borton, "Recent Trends in the International Relief System," *Disasters*, 17 (3) (1993).

[9] According to the World Food Program (WFP), NGOs share of food aid has increased significantly over the last 10 years or so, from 9.76 percent to 20.96 percent between 1988 and 1994.

[10] This relies, admittedly, on partial, mostly incomplete data in categories that are somewhat poorly defined or which various sources define in different ways—"emergency aid," "humanitarian aid," "NGO," etc. Moreover, these figures are based solely on government funding channeled through NGOs and do not include the often appreciable private funding these organizations attract. Research is needed to better evaluate, for each crisis, the volume of funding raised and basic categories of usage (food or other material aid, transport, local expenditures, local employees, services, etc.). The problem of obtaining trustworthy, comprehensive data is partly due to the complex and fragmentary nature of the system of emergency aid; more than anything else it reflects the comparative absence of transparency in the international aid system where, despite the vast sums involved, accountability is still a relative concept.

the attendant downside of sustaining ruling power clienteles and raising the stakes for conquering the state apparatus and getting a piece of the national "pie." Since the 1980s, these state "networks" have been largely short-circuited as development aid has diminished, first in favor of structural readjustment strategies that in many cases led to partial privatization of public services;[11] later the emphasis moved to emergency aid increasingly channeled via private entities. This bypassing of the state, inspired by policies promoting economic privatization and support for "civil society," is especially conspicuous in the sphere of emergency aid, which by its very nature calls for rapid distribution to needy populations and is also highly vulnerable to manipulation in conflict situations, where it represents enormous spoils for warring parties. In the mid-1980s certain donors such as the United States indicated their desire to establish, if not an exclusive, then at least a privileged relationship with NGOs to implement relief operations. This was later extended to the majority of donor nations, European countries chief among them.

No longer is the state the preferred channel for international aid in conflict-ridden countries. But this reexamination of the role states play has not meant their exclusion from the networks of emergency aid, for three reasons.

First, in beneficiary countries, states are still the preferred interlocutors of the international community. They profit, often quite lucratively, from allowing relief agencies to intervene in zones outside state control.[12] Weakened though they may be, states retain significant assets that allow them to turn relief operations conducted in their territory to their advantage. Despite the need for impartiality, aid providers, particularly UN intergovernmental agencies, are in fact often straitjacketed by political constraints that force them either to bow to pressure from national authorities or, in the absence of any serious needs assessment—or out of

---

[11] Béatrice Hibou, "Capital Social et l'État Falsificateur" [Social Capital and the Fraudulent State], in J.-F. Bayart, S. Ellis and B. Hibou, *La Criminalisation de l'Etat en Afrique* [The Criminalization of the State in Africa] (Complexe, 1997).

[12] For example, until relative parity was achieved in Sudan in 1993, three-quarters of the aid funneled into the country was distributed within government zones, despite extensive needs in zones controlled by the SPLA. See Millard Burr and Robert Collins, *Requiem for the Sudan: War, Drought and Disaster Relief on the Nile* (Westview Press, 1995).

concern for "neutrality"—to implement relief operations in conflict zones solely on the basis of equal distribution among the warring parties. This dictate of balance clearly is a significant factor in the expansion of the aid market, especially given that the interests of local ruling powers and the institutional needs of aid agencies frequently coincide in terms of media visibility and how much relief can be obtained. At the end of the day, when humanitarian aid is distributed, it must be negotiated through, and monitored by, local rulers, national authorities, and armed movements, and this unquestionably contributes to the politicization of aid.

Second, donor countries have not remained passive. Western countries have gradually moved into the humanitarian sphere, which initially had come into being on an independent basis. As principal donors, they play a key role in decisions to intervene and, with legitimate reason, seek to make humanitarian action work in their interest. Humanitarian action is a weapon in a state's arsenal, as demonstrated once again by the United States' and France's maneuverings during the Zairian crisis of the winter of 1996–97. And intergovernmental entities in the UN system still play a central role in coordinating relief. With the emergence of "state humanitarianism,"[13] there seems to be a new willingness among some donor countries to intervene on the ground in media-covered crises in an effort to heighten their visibility by implementing their own relief programs.[14] This new activism on the part of government aid agencies is still in its early days, but the growing power of ECHO is testimony, in the European context, to the presence of new donors in the now highly coveted humanitarian arena.

Finally, this reorientation of the emergency aid system in favor of private actors has its ambiguities: the label "nongovernmental" is a poor descriptor given the diverse nature of interactions between NGOs and civil or military state actors. The growing share of government funding in NGO

---

[13] As demonstrated by France's appointment of a Secretary of State for Humanitarian Action in 1998 or the creation, in 1992, of the European Commission's Humanitarian Aid Office (ECHO) and the UN's Department of Humanitarian Affairs (DHA).

[14] Some donor nations are beginning to field operations units. After the relief operation for the Kurdish Refugees in April-May 1991, the British international aid agency (ODA) created Disaster Relief Teams, which intervened in Iraq and later in Bosnia. ECHO has an operations wing as well, the European Community Task Force (ECTF), which directly executes certain European relief programs in Croatia and Bosnia.

budgets[15] raises fundamental questions about the status of these organizations; some remain autonomous actors inclined to formulate their own strategies, while others are no more than subcontractors for donors, pure and simple.[16] This growing dependence of many NGOs with respect to government funding is even more problematic, because in certain situations a supply-side political dynamic is emerging that motivates donor countries to intervene for political or media-related motives.[17] And a complex system of delegation and subcontracting is, in fact, gradually taking shape, involving a multitude of governmental, intergovernmental, and nongovernmental actors.

Nevertheless, state-to-state channels are now being exploited by new actors and networks that eclipse them and jeopardize their existence. Generally speaking, we have gone from a state-to-state system, essentially organized around political considerations, to a more open dynamic based on complex interactions among a variety of actors with highly diverse—if not contradictory—perceptions, modes of intervention, organizational cultures, and political, social, and economic goals.

"Internalizing" Humanitarian Aid

During the 1970s and 1980s humanitarian aid was nearly non-existent in full-blown crisis situations. Western countries, even those that most actively supported warring parties politically and financially, maintained a prudent distance from conflict zones; any direct intervention on their part, even in the guise of humanitarian aid, would have been perceived as interference and triggered an immediate response on the part of the states concerned or of their patron superpower. UN agencies, for their part, were in the main committed to "development" programs. They recoiled at the notion of involving themselves in full-blown crisis situations. In addition, their adherence

---

[15] Government funding represented 1.5% of NGO budgets in 1975, 35% in 1988, and most likely over 50% today ...; in Antonio Donini, "The Bureaucracy and the Free Spirits," *Third World Quarterly*, vol. 16, no. 3 (1995).

[16] Michael Edwards and David Hume, "Too Close for Comfort? The Impact of Official Aid on Nongovernmental Organizations," *World Development*, vol. 24, no. 6 (1996).

[17] Rony Brauman, *Humanitaire, le Dilemme* [The Dilemma of the Humanitarian Movement] (Textuel, 1996).

to the principle of sovereignty, maintained in the UN charter and scrupulously respected within that international organization, made it impossible for them to intervene in internal conflicts without the consent of the respective national authorities. As a result, up until the early 1980s the International Committee of the Red Cross (ICRC) was, in spite of its self-imposed limitations, the only organization actually present on the ground. At that time a new generation of non-state actors—personified in France by the "sans frontières" movement—began to breech the principle of sovereignty and intervene in conflict-ridden countries.[18] Such organizations were fairly rare, however, and until the start of the 1990s, contested zones of sovereignty, not to mention "rebel" zones, were virtually beyond the reach of international aid.

In the 1970s and 1980s, therefore, the often sizeable aid mobilized by Western nations and channeled via governmental, intergovernmental, or nongovernmental organizations was kept out of conflict-ridden countries and for the most part distributed in refugee camps.[19] In the 1980's climate of ideological nostalgia (for example: "freedom fighter"="good"; "guerilla fighter"="bad") Western nations further increased their support for refugee camps set up on the borders of conflict-ridden countries. This humanitarian aid—distinct, in theory, from political and military aid and distributed to armed movements through separate channels—had a sharp impact on war economies. In many cases refugee camps became "humanitarian sanctuaries"[20] and contributed to the perpetuation of conflicts; many armed movements acquired political legitimacy in camps by reason of their influence over refugee populations, secured an economic base via the international aid that poured in, and gained a source of fighters. Afghan or Pakistani refugee camps, the sites controlled by the "contras" in Honduras or the Khmer Rouge on the Thailand border—or, more

---

[18] Mark Duffield and John Prendergast, *Without Troops and Tanks, Humanitarian Intervention in Ethiopia and Eritrea* (The Red Sea Press, 1994).

[19] Afghanistan is a case in point: while aid distributed in refugee camps valued $400 million a year on average during the second half of the 1980s, aid funneled into the interior of the country during the same period by organizations operating across the border illegally amounted to only $20 million a year. See H. Baitenmann, "NGOs and the Afghan War, the Politicization of Humanitarian Aid," *Third World Quarterly*, 12 (1) (1990).

[20] Jean-Christophe Rufin, *Le Piège Humanitaire* [The Humanitarian Trap], J.C. Lattès (1986), (reedited, Hachette-Pluriel, 1993).

recently, the Rwandan refugee camps in Tanzania and Zaire—are all good illustrations of how armed movements manipulate refugee aid.[21]

The situation has evolved a great deal since the early 1990s: humanitarian aid, which played only a marginal role and was distributed only along the periphery of conflicts, now plays a central role in the dynamics of a conflict. As the importance of humanitarian aid in crisis situations increases, a profound transformation in the process of distribution is also occurring: it is spreading inwards from the periphery towards the center of conflicts. With the end of the Cold War, humanitarian aid is no longer distributed only in refugee camps: it is increasingly being channeled to the interior of conflict-ridden countries, into the heart of combat zones. To be sure, the overall situation is not radically different, if only because refugees continue to flee countries in crisis and "humanitarian sanctuaries" are still a pressing issue—as the case of the Rwandan refugee camps demonstrates ... Still, the rigid separation between combat zones located inside countries in crisis and sites where aid is distributed, in border regions, is beginning to disappear, and the aid system is increasingly operating deep within conflict zones. This process of "internalizing" humanitarian aid is linked to two kinds of factors.

To begin with, states now have broader latitude for intervention in internal conflicts where the "ideological" explanations so cherished during the Cold War have yielded place to "ethnic" explanations that are politically neutral and supply moral incentive for outside intervention. In addition, the United Nations, long paralyzed by East-West confrontation, has become a vehicle of hope for many and has attempted to play a role in "peacekeeping." The euphoria was short-lived: the hazards of "peacekeeping operations" only underline the difficulty of international interventions in internal crisis situations. As for "military-humanitarian" interventions, these continue to be pursued on a selective and expedient basis, depending upon media visibility, political significance, and the pressure of public opinion. Six years after the intervention launched in northern Iraq and four years after the Somalia fiasco in 1993—the high-water

---

[21] On the Khmer refugee camps in Thailand, see William Shawcross, *The Quality of Mercy* (Touchstone Books, Revised Edition November 1985).

mark of "humanitarian intervention"—the hesitancy of Western nations to confront the crisis in Kivu is confirmation of their increasing reluctance to become involved in full-blown crises of no obvious political importance. Despite their mixed record of success, these interventions have, nonetheless, gradually accustomed state and international actors to the notion of intervening in countries beset by conflict.

The principle of national sovereignty is still generally accepted, but is now undergoing a complex process of redefinition and, in crises focused on by the media, is sometimes contested out of a concern to protect threatened populations. As a result, an increasing number of states have had to resign themselves to authorizing humanitarian operations within their territory, including conflict zones. The rapidly increasing number of relief programs based on the concepts of "humanitarian corridors" and negotiated access is evidence of this change. Operation Lifeline Sudan (OLS), launched in April 1989, was the first relief operation UN agencies carried out in conflict zones to be based on a negotiated accord between the two warring parties. This new type of operation, which was reproduced in 1990 in Angola, 1991 in Iraq, 1992 in Bosnia, and elsewhere, constitutes a legitimization—made official in the course of innumerable UN Security Council resolutions—of the kind of cross-border operations in zones of contested sovereignty that until now had been conducted only by NGOs. UN agencies, which traditionally had only intervened after the conclusion of a cease-fire or the signing of a peace accord, are now increasingly involved in crisis areas.[22]

This inclination to intervene directly in crisis zones is reinforced still more by changes in refugee policy over recent years.[23] Refugees, who enjoyed political significance and a positive public image during the Cold War era, are now viewed as undesirables. As a result Western nations try to avoid new refugee flows across international borders. For this purpose the international "community" tries as often as possible to keep displaced

---

[22] Up to that point UNICEF had been the only UN program which, as per its mandate, was permitted to intervene in zones of contested sovereignty without the prior agreement of national authorities or in countries where the government had not been recognized by the international community, as was the case in Cambodia between 1979 and 1992.

[23] François Jean, "Le Fantôme des Réfugiés" [The Spectre of Refugees], *Esprit* (December 1992).

populations within crisis-ridden countries, in zones protected (theoretically) by an international presence and supplied (in principle) by relief convoys. The main aim of Operation Provide Comfort was to persuade afflicted Kurds to stay away from the Turkish border and return to their homes by offering them temporary protection and humanitarian aid in northern Iraq. Together with the Bosnian intervention, this was a remarkable example of the new three-part policy of containment—or even push back—based on repatriation, humanitarian corridors, and security zones. From Iraq to Yugoslavia, including Rwanda, this new policy is coming more widely into practice. No longer is humanitarian aid distributed only in refugee camps on the periphery of conflict zones. Increasingly, it is dispatched within crisis-ridden countries, in the heart of combat zones.

This "internalization" of international initiatives means that humanitarian assistance is now being delivered in the very midst of a conflict dynamic. In a financial sense, first of all, because money is quite often the only resource still infused into internal conflicts that no longer inspire any real interest on the part of foreign powers. But also in a geographic sense, because the model of "humanitarian sanctuary" is yielding more and more to that of the "security zone."

The Role of Humanitarian Aid in Conflict Dynamics

The developments broadly outlined above have introduced a situation utterly unique in the history of warfare—conflict zones permeated by a multitude of international organizations. The status of these organizations is highly diverse—governmental, intergovernmental or nongovernmental—and quite often fairly ambiguous: "military-humanitarian"; governmental, but without precise objectives; private, but dependent on government funding; non-state actors involved in diplomatic processes ... These are organizations that engage not only in humanitarian action but also in areas such as peacekeeping, promoting human rights, conflict prevention or resolution, and more. They attract considerable amounts of funding, and their presence alone changes the nature of the game by introducing new factors. Humanitarian action is not merely a resource to be exploited by warring parties. It also serves as a constraint for all the parties to a conflict: it opens the dynamic up by depriving states of some of their prerogatives and establishing new linkages with the international system, and it reconfigures this state of play in the course of complex interactions built up between humanitarian actors and political-military movements or military-economic entrepreneurs. Clearly these are the dynamics we need to understand as we go back and examine each of these individual arenas of conflict.

Even if we exclude "military-humanitarian" interventions, humanitarian action is now part of the landscape of conflict—part of the dynamic of violence.[24] Despite the decline—and it has been a steep one since 1993, the high-water mark of "humanitarian intervention"—in international initiatives to offer relief and protection to civilian populations victimized by violence, it is rare for countries to openly oppose international relief operations. The case of Algeria is unique in this respect; it is a rare example of a conflict inaccessible both to humanitarian organizations and the international media. It is all the more atypical in that Algeria's civil war is playing out near Europe, pulling together all the elements (Islamization, terrorism, potential migrations, etc.) that have fueled the rhetoric of the "Southern Hemisphere threat" since the beginning of the 1990s ... Yet no Western country or humanitarian organization will take the risk of intervening. In addition to the issue of noninterference—the traditional objection, endlessly reasserted in this case by punctilious officials—the intense climate of insecurity has discouraged any international presence for a number of years. Such a situation remains the exception, however, as demonstrated by the contrary example of Russia. In spite of the country's long tradition of inaccessibility and government paranoia, the Kremlin and the army were obliged to tolerate the presence of non-state Western actors (journalists and humanitarian organizations) during a war of secession on the Russian Federation's own territory. While foreign governments—with the exception of one mission from the Organization for Security and Cooperation in Europe—and UN agencies were kept away from the conflict, portrayed as an internal Russian issue, the ICRC and a few NGOs were nonetheless able to operate deep inside conflict zones. The intervention was not without its difficulties, to be sure. Relief entities had to over-

---

[24] Mark Duffield, "NGO Relief in War Zones: Towards an Analysis of the New Aid Paradigm," *Third World Quarterly*, vol. 18, no. 3 (1997).

come all kinds of obstacles and faced overt political obstruction[25] before critical security issues (murders and kidnappings) forced them to leave the country. Nevertheless, the fact that they were able to intervene at all in such a context demonstrates how hard it has become for governments to oppose granting humanitarian actors access to conflict zones.

Gone are the days when adherence to the principle of sovereignty or respect for a state's desire to prohibit any aid inside "rebel" zones made access to conflict-ridden countries impossible or confined the aid market to the precincts of the ruling powers, as in Afghanistan, Sudan, or Angola. Still, humanitarian organizations are continually hampered by political obstacles and security constraints. It is important not to oversimplify here: when humanitarian actors encounter difficulties, it is not always due to a set purpose—still less a strategy—to keep them away from conflict zones. Even in countries where deliberate political obstacles are obvious, such as Algeria or Russia, the critical security problems that confront humanitarian organizations seem to stem more from a loss of control by the state, an increasing number of militarized actors, and spreading violence. In the case of countries like Somalia and Liberia, where the state has collapsed and armed groups have splintered, it is all the more difficult to speak of an intentional approach or deliberate strategy, at least not at the national level. Nevertheless, manipulating the security environment is, for certain groups in certain regions, a way of regulating the activities of international actors. In some cases, and particularly in areas with a heavy international presence, strategies have focused on dealing with the problem a foreign presence poses.

The African Great Lakes region, exposed to an overinvestment of humanitarian aid in recent years, provides a remarkable illustration of how local actors adapt their strategies. It is a particularly stark one, as well, because it had a clearly defined, limited focus—the "humanitarian sanctuaries" established in July 1994 along the Rwandan border. The November 15, 1996 attack on the Mugunga camp and the later return of hundreds of thousands of refugees to Rwanda played a decisive role in the cancel-

---

[25] François Jean, "The Problems of Medical Relief in the Chechen War Zone," *Central Asian Survey*, vol. 15, no. 2 (1996).

lution of the military humanitarian intervention in Kivu, which was being discussed at the time in international forums. Clearly the dispersal of the camps, which had been financed with humanitarian aid for the previous two years and had become rear-area camps for ex-FAR [Armed Forces of Rwanda] members, was in itself a goal for the new Rwandan authorities. Still, the possibility cannot be ruled out that the attack was part of a strategy explicitly aimed at preempting and preventing international intervention, as some of Paul Kagame's statements have in fact implied.[26] If that was the case, we witnessed a remarkable instance of Rwandan rulers factoring the dilemmas of humanitarian action into their strategy. In the few years since the wave of interventions at the beginning of the decade, some local actors appear to have mastered the syntax of "international community" action well enough to be able to discreetly pull the plug on an intervention sequence—to the great satisfaction of some Western countries reluctant to become involved or willing to let a power struggle play itself out ... In the case of the ex-Zaire, the specific issue, regardless of the humanitarian trappings, clearly had more to do with the problems of military intervention than those of the relief operation. In this respect it more closely recalls the October 1983 attacks perpetrated in Lebanon to compel the departure of the multinational force than it does the murder, ordered in certain Russian or Chechen circles, of six ICRC workers in Chechnya in December 1996—most likely aimed at forcing out the international presence prior to the oncoming elections. The difference was that, in the case of Zaire, the "rebels" did not go after the international actors. They "resolved" the humanitarian question that was the stated reason for the intervention—the protection of refugees—in order to deter a potential international intervention. Nevertheless, the November 1996 events in Kivu showed that local actors can learn from ongoing events: at a time when it appears difficult to overtly oppose international initiatives seeking to protect and deliver relief to threatened populations, they have been able to adjust their strategies and retake the initiative.

Such cases remain the exception, however, if only because they feature a

---

[26] "The Great Escape," *Economist*, November 23, 1996; "Rwandans Led Revolt in Congo," *The Washington Post*, July 9 1997.

dominant state actor pursuing a coherent strategy. In the majority of crises the security environment is manipulated on a sporadic and selective basis. The parties to the conflict seek not to prohibit the presence or operations of international organizations on national territory as a whole but rather to deter them or, on the contrary, to encourage them to intervene in such-and-such a region, depending on the political configuration and power relationships at the local level. Any international intervention in a conflict situation inspires innumerable, highly diverse, and sometimes contradictory initiatives to hinder relief or exploit it, avoid an international presence or facilitate it, erect a barrier or connect to the international system, and so on. These various competing strategies among armed factions, which international actors do not observe passively, target the economic, as well as the political and symbolic, spoils of aid in conflict-ridden countries and unfold far beyond their borders. Generally speaking, the strategies of local actors can be classified in two main categories: those centered around the economic resource humanitarian aid represents and those concentrated on the international presence in conflict zones.

Privatizing Public Services

The relative impact of aid as an economic resource depends on the extent of donor involvement and the volume of aid, as well as on the economy of the country where it is deployed and the nature of the crisis. A distinction can be made between long-term conflicts, where the society has been profoundly de-structured and aid is just as vital a resource for the warring parties as it is for the general population (particularly in African conflicts), and situations in which aid is one resource among others—whether in acute crises (Bosnia, Afghanistan, Peru, etc.) or periods of "transition" (Cambodia, Iraqi Kurdistan, etc.). Still, even in Africa there is a clear east-west cleavage between countries long-dependent on external assistance (Sudan, Somalia, Ethiopia, Mozambique) and countries that possess raw materials for export (Sierra Leone, Liberia, the ex-Zaire, Angola). Beyond such general distinctions, the impact of aid as a resource clearly depends on local circumstances: aid is all the more vital as a resource when it is deployed in conditions of scarcity or isolation, such as when civilian populations are cut off or under siege.

In any event, aid is a major resource that political and economic actors seek to appropriate and exploit for their own objectives. States and armed movements employ a wide variety of tactics to turn the aid windfall to their advantage, from taxation to intimidation and coercion. Even in a weakened condition, states possess important assets that enable them to reap advantage from relief operations conducted on their territory. Some administrative functions—setting exchange rates, for example—generate sizeable commissions, and state control over structures of access to the international channels where goods and services circulate yields substantial import-tax revenues. In many conflicts, therefore, armed movements vie for control of cities, ports, and airports—or the creation of new facilities—which permit them to bypass the state's monopoly on dealings with the outside world. Apart from taxation, a variety of forms of coercion and intimidation also exist, from the diversion of funds to plunder, including protection rackets.[27] Such practices enter in at every stage in the chain of aid delivery and are especially predominant in "insecurity zones," which afford excellent opportunities of this kind that are exploited by armies and armed movements alike. Practices of intimidation and coercion do not target humanitarian aid alone; they focus most heavily on civilian populations. In the new war economies, the delivery of humanitarian aid constantly replenishes the breeding ground for such abuses, allowing warring parties to sustain themselves with commissions or by diverting resources.

However, in spite of the violent nature of these types of efforts to seize the windfall of external aid, war economies do not operate on the basis of abuse and coercion alone. In many cases armed movements—though they may not correspond to the traditional model of guerilla fighters serving the common good—do enjoy a degree of legitimacy, sometimes based on mobilization along political, ethnic, or religious lines. Some movements may reinforce this legitimacy by their capacity to provide social services, or at least a social safety net, to civilians under their control as compensation for material exactions or rights abuses such as forced conscription or

---

[27] Stephen Ellis, "Liberia 1989-1994; A Study of Ethnic and Spiritual Violence," *African Affairs*, no. 94 (1995).

labor.[28] Humanitarian aid becomes a major resource, as a result, because it legitimizes protection rackets and, consequently, the power of states and armed opposition movements.[29] While this legitimizing function is often more important than the social objective, strictly speaking, international aid supplies do give warring parties the means to offer services to the civilian populations in areas they control.[30] In weak or weakened states such as Afghanistan, Somalia, Liberia, or Bosnia, or in zones controlled by armed movements such as southern Sudan, northern Iraq, or the Angolan interior, aid entities help to preserve or reintroduce minimal public services and institutional capacities by providing employment for the educated and keeping some social services functioning. In so doing they help to maintain or reestablish the rudiments of civil administration—but in a decentralized, even incoherent way, because their activities cover both guerilla zones and zones controlled by internationally recognized authorities. In this respect humanitarian action is actually neutral in impact. Depending on the circumstances, the configuration of the conflict, and the actors' strategies, it may help to strengthen a state or the reverse—it may weaken a state when it supports the social initiatives of factions trying to set themselves up as rival states by assuming responsibilities traditionally discharged by central authorities.

How extensive an impact humanitarian aid has, in this respect, largely depends on the conflict's protagonists: how they are organized, their relations with civilian populations, and their political agendas. In Somalia and Liberia, for example, many factions appear not to have tried to utilize aid resources to enhance their own legitimacy. But in most conflicts armed

---

[28] François Jean, "Aide Humanitaire et Économie de Guerre" [Humanitarian Aid and the Economics of War], in *Économie des Guerres Civiles* [The Economics of Civil Wars], eds. F. Jean and J. C. Rufin (Fondation pour les Études de Défense, Hachette-Pluriel, 1996).

[29] Charles. Tilly, "War Making and State Making as Organized Crime," in *Bringing the State Back In*, eds. P. Evans, D. Rueschemeyer and T. Skocpol (Cambridge University Press, 1985).

[30] When hostilities were renewed in Angola in 1993, for example, humanitarian aid made it possible to keep minimal public services up and running, both for the government side— then engaged in economic reforms that called for deep cutbacks in social expenditures— and for UNITA, which suffered serious financial setbacks after foreign support, South Africa's in particular, had been cut off. See Alex Vines, ed., *Angola: Arms Trade and Violations of the Laws of War since the 1992 Elections* (Human Rights Watch/Africa, 1994); and Alex de Waal, *Humanitarianism Unbound?* African Rights, discussion paper no. 5 (1994).

movements do attempt to manipulate aid from abroad to consolidate
their power, using strategies that vary in degree of sophistication. The
least-organized movements are satisfied with authorizing an NGO to operate on their territory, simply claiming its achievements as their own and
taking credit for them to burnish their reputations among civilian populations. From Sudan to Afghanistan, there is no doubt that building a hospital or a clinic enhances the prestige and influence of the local boss, who
can boast of his ability to tap the windfall of external aid for his people's
benefit. The better organized movements, or those most focused on their
relations with civilian populations, go beyond traditional, clientelist strategies and associating themselves symbolically with international aid. They
seek to build legitimacy and secure their influence over civilian populations by rebuilding administrative capacity and implementing redistributive policies.

Often these initiatives come wrapped in humanitarian packaging—most
armed movements in fact have a humanitarian wing. These NGOs, created
by political-military movements, are part of a remarkable flourishing of
local NGOs currently operating in Southern Hemisphere countries. But
this movement by political-military actors into the humanitarian sphere in
countries beset by conflict is not, for the most part, internally generated; it
often occurs in response to the expectations of actors within the aid system,
with its current rhetoric promoting "civil society," "capacity building," and
support for local NGOs. Donors are reassured by this façade of neutrality,
and armed movements are thus in a better position to garner international
funding. In some cases local NGOs truly have the ability to act and possess
some degree of independence from ruling powers. In others they are mere
humanitarian "window dressing," wholly subordinate to military authority,
as is the case in southern Sudan or Sri Lanka. In the conflicts in Lebanon
and Eritrea during the 1970s and 1980s, or those continuing now in Angola
or in Sri Lanka, some armed movements have sought to arrogate the state's
functions to themselves, setting up civil administrations to provide minimal
social services with respect to education and health or to ensure the distribution of supplies to the neediest. At times the rough outlines of a movement towards privatizing "public services" through an aid process based
on the current triangle of donors, international NGOs, and non-state local

actors seem to be emerging; this further weakens states already struggling to cope with the loss of their monopoly over violence and revenue raising.[31]

These developments reflect underlying changes that are readily discernible at the international level. All indicators are that we are witnessing the global spread of a parallel system of social welfare. In Western nations the erosion of the welfare state proceeds in the form of increasingly privatized social protections, mixed with specific government measures—largely charity oriented—for those left behind. Likewise, in Southern Hemisphere countries where structural adjustment plans advocated by the International Monetary Fund have encouraged policies of economic *laissez-faire*, the social-welfare component is in large measure being left to NGOs. In crisis situations this trend towards internationalization and privatization is still more pronounced. The responsibility for implementing a minimal safety net for those most at risk is increasingly subcontracted out to a host of international institutions, humanitarian organizations, and local associations.[32]

But states are not always passive spectators of developments such as these, which weaken the bonds between government and the governed and benefit armed movements that use humanitarian action to boost societal support and legitimacy. Some governments continue to assert sovereignty over their national territory as a whole by assuming responsibility for public services even in contested zones of sovereignty. In Sri Lanka the government continued to pay civil servants and to finance schools and hospitals on the Jaffna peninsula between 1990 and 1996, a period when the Liberation Tigers of Tamil Eelam (LTTE) nonetheless ruled alone in that part of the country. In other countries, national authorities are trying to thwart the mounting influence of Western NGOs. In Sudan, for example, the government is trying to promote and sustain Islamist NGOs such as Da'wa Islamiya and the Islamic Relief Agency (IARA) in order to increase its control over both Western-NGO activity and the civil-

---

[31] Mark Duffield, "The Emergence of Two-Tier Welfare in Africa: Marginalization or an Opportunity for Reform?" *Public Administration and Development*, vol. 12 (1992).

[32] François Jean, "L'humanitaire Irresponsable?" [Is the Humanitarian Movement Irresponsible?], *Agora*, no. 36 (fall 1995).

ian populations in zones retaken by government forces.[33] Finally, in some cases governments are directly attempting to reoccupy the public/social sphere that had to some degree slipped from their grasp and to reassert their authority. In Eritrea, Ethiopia, and Rwanda, the policies of the new authorities show a clear intent to limit the role of international NGOs and confine it to a framework determined by government authorities. What makes this development noteworthy is that the leaders of these three countries emerged from armed movements that acquired a good deal of experience with NGOs over years of war. Now in power, they appear to have studied the impact of humanitarian aid well and have adapted their strategies accordingly in order to regain the initiative.

Parallel Diplomacy

The growing presence of international actors in arenas of conflict has profound implications with respect to image building, legitimacy, and public support at the international level.

Since its beginnings, the humanitarian movement has had a close, symbiotic association with the media, from the creation of the Red Cross at the end of the 19th century during the first communications revolution (press-telegraph-railroads) to the triumph of the humanitarian movement at the dawn of the era of instant communications. During the Biafran conflict at the end of the 1960s, humanitarian action spread to the third world at the same time as televisions began to spring up in European living rooms. All along the way the media's evolution has paralleled the ascent of the humanitarian movement. The humanitarian project needs the media in order to focus the public's attention and mobilize support; the media relies on humanitarian actors when it covers distant crises. The presence of humanitarian organizations on the ground facilitates media coverage of a conflict, providing journalists with logistical facilities and news sources, as well as witness-interpreters of the same nationality to help them connect with TV viewers.[34] By virtue of its links to the media and the public opinion, the humanitarian movement has a vital poten-

---

[33] Jérôme Bellion-Jourdan, "L'Humanitaire et l'Islamisme Soudanais" [The Humanitarian Movement and Sudanese Islamicism], *Politique Africaine*, no. 66 (June 1997).

[34] Rony Brauman, "Comment les Médias Viennent aux Crises ?" [What Makes the Media Cover Crises?], in *Populations en Danger* 1995 [Populations in Danger 1995] (La Découverte, 1995).

tial for influencing a conflict's visibility and how much interest it will attract. The more highly organized armed movements are fully aware of this and have long sought to induce, or at the very least assist, humanitarian organizations to set up operations in territories under their control. In the 1970s and 1980s, many armed opposition movements such as UNITA [National Union for Total Independence of Angola] in Angola and the FPLE [Popular Front for the Liberation of Eritrea] in Eritrea guaranteed the security of humanitarian organizations. Throughout the Cold War the alliance of the stethoscope and the camera, a hallmark of the humanitarian movement, undoubtedly gave a higher profile to a number of movements seeking international recognition and legitimacy, allowing them to mobilize political and financial resources, or build support networks in Western countries.[35]

But the impact of the humanitarian movement is not limited to this "megaphone effect"; the movement also influences the intensity and the interpretive slant of the spotlight it shines on a conflict's protagonists. Indeed, many humanitarian organizations pursue an active policy of bearing witness to crises—to the point, at times, of denouncing local authorities. Bolstered by their media intermediaries and the public's response, the positions taken by humanitarian organizations often have an important influence on how conflicts are construed and warring parties perceived. The events of the past 20 years—from the exodus of the Vietnamese boat people to the Rwandan genocide, as well as the Afghan, Ethiopian, and Bosnian wars, among others—testify eloquently to the impact that humanitarian involvement has had on evolving perceptions in Western countries and its role in mobilizing public opinion in democratic countries. In this respect, Biafra is clearly the foremost example of the impact of humanitarian aid in terms of recognition as well as international mobilization in aid of an armed movement—all the more remarkable in that, when Biafran leaders failed to sell their cause to the international public, they tried compassion, peddling their victims instead.[36]

Emerging from the Cold War, this "strategic victimhood" is more of an issue than ever. With the East-West confrontation at an end, the defense

---

[35] The case of Commander Massoud in Afghanistan is an excellent example in this respect.

[36] Rony Brauman, *L'Action Humanitaire* [Humanitarian Action] (Flammarion, 1995).

of human rights has taken the place of ideological orientation, the consequences of human conflict have returned to the foreground, and playing
the humanitarian card is more of an asset than ever in the process of building legitimacy by focusing attention on victims. As humanitarian organizations strive to focus attention on overlooked tragedies, defend threatened
populations, and denounce rights abuses, political-military forces—
deprived of their traditional sources of support—have had to adapt to the
new language of international relations in order to garner support and consolidate power. From Sudan to Afghanistan, states and armed movements
seek to exploit the fate of civilian populations either to lure or latch onto
international assistance, to legitimize themselves or discredit their adversaries, and more. Many varieties of strategic victimhood are practiced in
arenas of conflict, some more sophisticated than others, but the better-orga-
nized groups most open to the outside world have been able to mobilize
humanitarian aid and rhetoric in service of their objectives. This doesn't
mean the maneuvering is confined only to warring parties trying to exploit
aid. It reflects complex interactions based on confrontation, cooperation,
or manipulation among local and international actors. And this web of
strategies is, naturally, part of an overall dynamic that unfolds in space and
time, shifting repeatedly as information circulates, elicits responses, modi-
fies perceptions, produces unintended consequences, etc., at the global
level. Positions and practices need to be continually readjusted in response
to these dynamic interactions. Some humanitarian organizations, alert to
practices of exploiting and manipulating aid, closely reexamine the impact
of their own activities and try to modify their methods of intervention so as
to limit any perverse effects. Likewise, some actors understand the limits of
humanitarian action and have responded by moving into the political realm
to challenge local authorities, call for international intervention, or partici-
pate in diplomatic initiatives.

  Humanitarian organizations do not limit themselves only to facilitating
media coverage of conflicts or raising international public awareness of
the plight of civilian populations and the rights abuses they suffer. They
are increasingly becoming policy advocates. And players in conflicts—
political-military leaders or military-economic entrepreneurs—are well
aware of this. Having courted and protected humanitarian actors through-

out the Cold War, using victimhood strategies to exploit their concern for threatened civilian populations, these actors now increasingly view them either as allies or enemies—as political actors with probable influence over international decisions (particularly regarding international interventions). The result has been a rapid increase in kidnappings and murders of members of humanitarian organizations in the past few years. This is an oversimplified picture, of course: it is no new thing for humanitarian organizations to lobby policymakers ... Nevertheless, in recent years they have grown far closer to official policymakers and sometimes have a significant influence on highly political questions such as decisions about whether or not to intervene. Humanitarian actors are playing an expanding political role and local rulers are ever more aware of the symbolic, economic, and political stakes involved in humanitarian action. This is so because a) conflicts stripped of strategic import for Western countries are increasingly perceived in terms of a humanitarian narrative, b) with political and financial support no longer available to warring parties, in many cases humanitarian aid is the last remaining external resource to be injected into conflict-ridden countries, and c) humanitarian action is sometimes the West's only response to political crises.

This increasing involvement on the part of humanitarian actors in policymaking with respect to conflicts reflects two kinds of processes at work. The first of these new developments is that, within the UN system, the boundaries between the domains of humanitarian action and international security have begun to dissolve. This greater permeability is partly a result of a heightened awareness of the issue of human rights, as I've mentioned previously. Gone are the days when massive human rights violations were considered to be strictly an internal, state matter. The erosion of the principle of sovereignty and a concern for stability have led the UN Security Council, in certain cases with a high media profile, to expand the collective security system to include internal conflicts. Resolution 688 of April 5, 1991, on Iraq established a link, for the first time, between events taking place within a state's borders and international peace and security in cases of widespread human rights violations that threaten to trigger refugee flows across international borders. It launched a long series of resolutions embracing humanitarian issues, rationales, and sometimes

even objectives. The humanitarian label has become a stamp of legitimacy for every political-military act or semblance of action. As a result,
humanitarian organizations are increasingly associated with policymaking.
This trend is especially pronounced within the UN system, which, despite
its state-to-state orientation, is one of the principle forums for interaction between governmental and nongovernmental actors. The much
commented-on participation and influence of NGOs at international
conferences in Rio, Beijing, and Istanbul are but the tip of the iceberg
in this regard.[37] While there are few formal procedures or institutional
frameworks that provide for NGO participation, a great number of informal channels have gradually been established that enable private actors
to interact with political authorities at the United Nations. As a result
the "traffic" of humanitarian issues coming before the Security Council
has become much heavier in recent years.[38] Humanitarian organizations
provide member states with information from the field on crises and
track the council's deliberations closely. Likewise, the delegate from the
International Red Cross in New York meets monthly with the council president, representatives of the principal. And humanitarian organizations
have regular access to the secretary-general. In many cases humanitarian actors become policy advocates and, in crises with no major strategic
import, may have significant influence in decision-making processes.
Member state representatives cannot ignore their close links with the
media and public opinion, and UN agencies have ongoing dealings and
maintain cooperative relationships with NGOs.[39]

These interactions are not confined to UN headquarters in New York;
they are part of a vast web of relationships being constructed between
conflict-ridden countries and Western capitals. Indeed, NGOs are increas-

---

[37] Marie-Claude Smouts, "La Construction Equivoque d'une Opinion Mondiale" [The Ambiguous
Construction of International Public Opinion]; Sophie Bessis, "Les Nouveaux Enjeux et les
Nouveaux Acteurs des Débats Internationaux dans les Années 90" [New Issues and New Actors
in International Debates of the 1990s], *Tiers Monde*, no. 151 (July-September 1997).

[38] Antonio Donini, op. cit.

[39] Moreover, the potential role for humanitarian organizations in conflict resolution was
explicitly acknowledged by Boutros Boutros-Ghali, then-UN secretary-general. In his
1992 book, *Agenda for Peace*, he cited "humanitarian diplomacy" based on the idea that
humanitarian aid could be one form of leverage for the return to peace.

ingly consulted and given heed in Western countries owing to their knowledge of the terrain and their proximity to civilian populations in conflict zones. This is already a well-established trend in the United States, where humanitarian organizations—American and non-American alike—have long engaged in intense lobbying of policy makers. They frequently testify at congressional hearings and are granted access to the State Department to press their points of view on crises where they are intervening. These practices are spreading in European countries as well, where NGOs have increasing access to policymaking authorities. Moreover, while these consultations remain informal in most instances, they sometimes involve institutional entities in charge of coordination and planning. France's Secretary of State for Humanitarian Action and Human Rights National Advisory Commission, the European Commission's Humanitarian Aid Office (ECHO), the UN's Department of Humanitarian Affairs and High Commissioner for Human Rights all represent new bridges between humanitarianism and politics. In conflict-ridden countries, as well, contacts with embassies are rapidly expanding, and humanitarian organizations active in sensitive zones are consulted frequently. The same is true of the increasingly numerous "special envoys" in crisis areas, who are in continuous contact with private actors that have experience in those zones. And armed forces on peacekeeping missions in conflict areas have created divisions for civil affairs—the better to manage their multifaceted interactions with humanitarian actors. The boundaries between humanitarian action and politics have grown progressively indistinct as these interactions continue to accumulate; even as states move into the humanitarian sphere, private actors are increasingly participating in political processes.

Above and beyond the mounting influence humanitarian actors exert on policymakers, a "parallel diplomacy" conducted by private actors has emerged in recent years. This expansion of the diplomatic arena is one of many profound changes occurring in diplomacy; chief among these is a greater diversity of negotiating channels (as demonstrated by Jimmy Carter's mediating role in Haiti, the Oslo process, and the negotiations over the Sudanese conflict in Addis Ababa under the aegis of the InterGovernmental Authority on Development (IGAD) and an ever growing number of official mediation efforts (as occurred during the Great

Lukcu regional crisis, where 10 special envoys were sent representing the
United Nations, the Organization of African Unity, the European Union,
the Arusha group, the United States, etc.).[40] In the latter context the
opening up of the diplomatic arena to include private actors constitutes a
new phase that reflects the aid market's expansion to include markets for
conflict mediation, resolution, and prevention: in light of the recurring
nature of humanitarian interventions and the hazards of peacekeeping
operations, some donors are looking for quick fixes that promise to prevent conflicts—cheaply and discreetly—from escalating.[41] This opening is
also driven by internal changes in humanitarian organizations that intervene in conflicts. Faced with the human consequences of crises and limits
on what their interventions can achieve, some organizations are searching for ways to alleviate the causes of conflicts. For example, a growing
number of humanitarian organizations—including human rights groups,
journalists' and church associations—have broadened their range of intervention to include conflict prevention, conciliation, or resolution at the
local level, and by lobbying at the international level as well. At the same
time specialized organizations have rapidly grown in number over the past
10 years (the Community of Sant'Edigio, the Carter Center, International
Alert, the International Crisis Group, etc.). These NGOs sometimes find
themselves acting in quasi-official roles. They are seated alongside other
players at negotiating tables, have direct access to policy makers and the
international media, have significant resources at their disposal, etc.
Nevertheless, with the exception of the Community of Sant'Egidio's success in Mozambique's peace process,[42] this infatuation with parallel diplomacy has not yielded convincing results up to now. The earliest analyses of
initiatives of this kind reveal a mixed record, to say the least.[43] The case of

---

[40] Likewise, Ahmedou Ould-Abdallah, the UN secretary-general's Special Representative in
Burundi, estimated that some 70 delegations had passed through the country between
November 1993 and January 1995.

[41] The principal donors in this area are the United States, the European Union, the
Scandinavian countries, and Japan, as well as some large American foundations.

[42] Cameron Hume, *Ending Mozambique's War* (United States Institute of Peace, 1994).

[43] Barnett R. Rubin ed., *Cases and Strategies for Preventive Action* (New York: The Century
Foundation Press, 1998).

Burundi, which over the past three years has served as the preferred testing ground for this kind of approach, is instructive: too many contradictory, individualized short term initiatives further fragmented the state of play politically, provoking a disarray that encouraged manipulation of all sorts. Local actors adapted to the new institutional landscape, playing one strategy off another while exploiting many of their interlocutors' inconsistencies and lack of long-term perspective. Each Burundian political faction found temporary allies among outside interventionists, who themselves became part of the problem in an atmosphere of media one-upmanship and competing strategies of victimhood.[44]

Be that as it may, the rise of parallel diplomacy is an illustration of how private actors are appropriating prerogatives heretofore wielded by states alone. Both in the diplomatic and civil service spheres, the developments currently unfolding in arenas of conflict are proof of the weakening of the state and the burgeoning role of non-state actors. Humanitarian organizations, to be sure, are not the sole private international actors intervening in conflict-ridden countries. They are but one example of the emergence and spreading of transnational networks that extend far beyond the borders of spaces of conflict, with profound impact on the dynamics of violence.

---

[44] Fabienne Hara, "La Diplomatie Parallèle ou la Politique de Non-Indifférence : le Cas du Burundi" [Parallel Diplomacy, or the Politics of Non-Indifference: The Case of Burundi], *Politique Africaine* no. 68 (December 1997). Didier Bigo, "Grands Débats Pour un Petit Monde" [Big Debates for a Small World], *Cultures et Conflits*, No. 19/20 (winter, 1995).

CHAPTER SEVENTEEN

Humanitarian Action: Image, Perception, and Security

Lisbon, Portugal; March 27-28, 1998

Principles for Humanitarian Action

Looting, kidnappings, murder ... For some years humanitarian organizations have faced mounting dilemmas when intervening in conflict situations. The (still unresolved) issue of the protection of victims has been compounded by the problem of security for volunteers and the national and international staff of relief organizations. The present forum on security comes at just the right moment, therefore, and I'd like to thank the European Commission's Humanitarian Aid Office (ECHO) and the International Committee of the Red Cross (ICRC) for offering an occasion to have a dialogue and reflect upon this issue that is so central to our concerns.

I've been asked to speak to the issue of guiding principles from the viewpoint of a nongovernmental organization, following up on the ICRC's presentation, and I'll be happy to do so. But first I'd like to frame these security issues in context. I will not discuss the real or alleged ways in which conflict situations have changed—this is a subject in itself, and it would take me far afield from the present topic. What I am going to look at instead, if only briefly, is how the system of aid has evolved over the course of the past decade. This is highly important, I believe, because the increase in security incidents has occurred in the context of a very rapid increase in the number of international actors present in conflict zones.

I'll begin by briefly describing developments in the system of aid over the last 10 years or so, highlighting what I think are the most relevant aspects for problems in security.

Then I'm going to address the topic of principles that guide the activities of humanitarian organizations, not just in terms of general philosophy, but trying to look at how these principles are expressed in concrete ways.

Redeploying Aid

Aid is now being redeployed, very broadly speaking, in two ways. There has been a substantial increase in government funding in the area of humanitarian aid and a growing role for nongovernmental organizations (NGOs) in its implementation. At the same time aid distribution is spreading inward from the peripheries to the centers of conflict zones.

Rapid and thoroughgoing changes have occurred in the dynamics of international aid over the last 10 years. As a result, development aid, pledged mainly within the framework of state-to-state relations, has given way to humanitarian aid, which is being implemented more and more by private entities, the NGOs.

All sources point to a significant expansion of humanitarian aid in proportion to total government-funded development aid, which has been on the decline since the end of the 1980s. In the case of ECHO alone, one of the largest donors in this field, the volume of emergency humanitarian aid grew sixfold between 1990 and 1994. Even as funding from governments appears to have stabilized or even decreased slightly since 1994, humanitarian aid seems to have become Western nations' response of choice to political crises of minor strategic significance.

The second major trend in this respect is that funding by governments, often substantial, is increasingly being channeled via private entities. Here again, to give only one example, ECHO directed at least half of its funding, on average, to NGOs between 1990 and 1994.

Of course this very rough outline needs to be qualified and fleshed out. Without going into too much detail, I'd like to add at least three caveats and point out a few recent developments.

- First, UN organizations remain very important actors and play a central, coordinating role at the nexus of politics and humanitarian action.
- Next, states haven't ceased to be active. They are increasingly moving into the humanitarian arena, which initially came into being independent of government involvement.
- Finally, the expanding share of government funding in NGO budgets raises fundamental questions as to the status of these organizations.

Some remain autonomous entities that tend to formulate their own strategies while others have become subcontractors for donors.

In addition, new entities are now emerging and attracting donor interest and support—organizations specializing in conflict prevention or resolution, as well as local NGOs.

I won't elaborate on these developments or comment on them. What I'd like to emphasize here is that humanitarian aid is now being channeled through a complex system of delegation and subcontracting that involves a multitude of governmental, intergovernmental, and nongovernmental entities.

In 10 years, generally speaking, we have gone from a state-to-state system, essentially grounded in political considerations, to a more open dynamic based on complex interactions among a number of actors with highly diverse, if not contradictory, perceptions, modes of intervention, organizational cultures, and political, social, and economic goals.

Alongside this institutional and political transformation—and this is the second point I wanted to make in this brief description of how the system of aid is changing—humanitarian aid is also becoming "internalized." By this crude term I mean the expansion of aid distribution from the periphery inwards towards the center of conflicts.

In the 1970s and 1980s humanitarian aid was almost nonexistent in conflict zones. For a series of reasons—Cold War constraints with respect to national sovereignty—the United Nations and individual states, even those most deeply involved as political and financial supporters of warring parties, did not undertake humanitarian intervention in countries at war.

Only the ICRC and a few NGOs intervened in nations in conflict. These organizations were more or less the exception, however, and the bulk of aid was delivered in refugee camps on the periphery of conflicts.

Since the early 1990s the situation has changed considerably. A whole set of factors upon which, again, I will not elaborate here—the erosion of the principle of sovereignty and new policy on refugees designed to avoid new refugee problems as much as possible while delivering aid to internally displaced populations in crisis-ridden countries—have led to an increasing number of humanitarian interventions in conflict zones.

These interventions may take different forms, but the increasing number of "military-humanitarian" operations such as Provide Comfort, Restore Hope, and, particularly, relief programs based on the idea of negotiated access such as Operation Lifeline Sudan have in a sense legitimized and institutionalized relief operations previously conducted only by NGOs in zones of contested sovereignty.

As a result, states and UN agencies are now to be found alongside NGOs in countries beset by crisis, sometimes in military roles. Humanitarian aid is no longer distributed only in refugee camps at the periphery of conflicts; it is now conveyed into countries in conflict by a multitude of international entities that at times intervene deep within combat zones.

These developments, which I'm afraid I have outlined here much too briefly, are creating a situation utterly unique in the history of warfare—conflict zones permeated by a multitude of international organizations.

The status of these organizations is highly diverse—governmental, inter-governmental, or nongovernmental—and quite often fairly ambiguous: "military-humanitarian"; private, but dependent on government funding; non-state actors involved in diplomatic processes, etc....

These are organizations that engage not only in humanitarian action but also in areas such as human rights, peacekeeping, conflict prevention or resolution, etc., and are often directly or indirectly involved in the political decision-making process.

Finally, these organizations attract considerable funding in conflict situations, where humanitarian aid at times is the last remaining resource Western nations will provide.

Humanitarian actors themselves sometimes find it difficult to orient themselves in this complex institutional environment, one that continually reconfigures itself in a somewhat confusing manner. This confusion is all the more understandable because it is abetted, consciously or not, by the deliverers of aid themselves: state actors who often claim the mantle of humanitarian action with the greatest conviction without stopping to consider their political responsibilities and humanitarian actors who, with the finest intentions in the world, at times turn into policy advocates and thereby add to the prevailing ambiguity.

In circumstances such as these it would be astonishing if local actors perceived humanitarian entities in an accurate way. And how humanitarian entities are perceived by local political-military leaders and local populations is clearly one of the key questions of the moment. It is a fundamental question for the future of humanitarian action. It is a central question, as well, when we reflect upon the security problems we now face.

In the absence of in-depth surveys in the major crisis zones, the question remains unresolved. But the impressions we have been able to gather on the ground would indicate that, at best, humanitarian organizations are viewed as importers of all-terrain vehicles—at worst as a new affluent class. Likewise, everything leads one to believe they are perceived either as agents of their governments or of the West—in any event as actors with political agendas and influence.

Part of this perception may be rooted in the trouble local actors sometimes have distinguishing among various entities—between state actors (civilian or military) and humanitarian actors—something that has occurred in certain zones exposed to large-scale international intervention—Somalia, for example. Paradoxically, at a time when political crises are seen more and more as complex "humanitarian emergencies," humanitarians themselves are increasingly perceived as political actors … As a consequence it isn't clear that military protection would enhance security for humanitarian aid workers—on the contrary, it could very well cast doubt on their independence and impartiality and diminish their capacity to intervene. It is essential for humanitarian actors to remain identifiable as such and to differentiate themselves as much as possible from political, and especially military, actors.

But it is doubtful whether this alone would solve the problem. Because it's not simply a matter of blurred boundaries. Conspiracy fantasies or theories notwithstanding—and sadly these are all too widespread in countries beset by conflict—at the end of the day warring parties do, in fact, have a broadly realistic appreciation of what humanitarian aid entails. They are not wrong, in any event, to view us collectively as having a political role or political influence.

The issue is not reducible to blurred boundaries alone—the real question is how international relations are being transformed: the expanding role of private actors, the increasing complexity of decision-making processes, and so on. I won't go into the changes currently unfolding in the international system; nevertheless it is clear that private entities are becoming ever more involved in political decision making. The heavier flow of humanitarian issues coming before the Security Council, to cite only one example, is an obvious sign of this.

Humanitarian organizations have political influence—there's no point in concealing it. We are better off recognizing and accepting it while attempting to better define our role, to work out more clearly what our responsibilities are. If we are to do this, we should first of all clarify our relationships with other actors in the relief system, both government and nongovernmental. This means reinforcing the ways in which we coordinate, the different areas in which we are complementary, and, most important, the dynamics at play when organizations of different types interact. Then we need to go back and reevaluate our practices, our methods of intervention, and our relations with populations. And this involves rethinking what we do and what our responsibilities are.

To illustrate a few of the issues we face I'm going to return to the idea of *advocacy*, which Madame Bonino very rightly emphasized just a moment ago.

Nowadays all humanitarian organizations, even those most committed to the idea of neutrality, engage in advocacy vis-à-vis political decision makers. But the term *advocacy* can apply to very different approaches, from bearing witness to promoting policies.

Some organizations believe it their duty to expose and even to denounce a political authority when they witness, or are sole witnesses to, rights abuses. Others try to lobby decision makers in favor of this or that policy and set themselves broader objectives, such as conflict prevention or resolution.

All of these approaches indisputably have political implications. But this doesn't necessarily mean they are part of a political project. What distinguishes humanitarian actors from political actors is that they are motivated by the victims' interest, not by political objectives.

The victims' interest is a key concept for humanitarian actors. But, again, it is a highly imprecise one that poses pitfalls for many. Too often one hears NGOs profess themselves to be the victims' representatives—this sort of claim to solidarity with a "brotherhood of victims" is, frankly, pathetic, even disturbing. Because it smacks of the very appropriately condemned "victimist" strategies used in some conflict zones by political-military leaders with a political or institutional interest in perpetuating the status of victims as victims.

The victim's interest rests squarely in no longer being a victim. Actions that are in the victims' interest are those which enable victims to escape that condition or that do not worsen their situation, in any case. The victims' interest might just as well call for dis-involvement as it does action, for either discreet silence or open denunciation, for politics or for humanitarian action. It cannot be defined in a general way, only case by case, in terms of a given situation and the opportunities it presents for action.

In any event, this is a basic issue that is a good example of how general concepts need to be re-clarified over and over again and that principles have no value unless they are continually reinterpreted in light of the issues we face on the ground when we intervene.

Having said that, I'd like to apologize in advance because I'm about to use some big words, *in abstracto*. I'm now going to address the question of principles, but given the format of this presentation I won't be able to tie them into concrete situations or problems to the extent I would wish. It goes without saying that I'm speaking to this issue from the point of view of one nongovernmental humanitarian organization; I speak on behalf of Médecins Sans Frontières (MSF).

Guiding Principles of Action

What are the principles that should guide us in this complex institutional environment, particularly in societies where we intervene?

Of course no principle, no philosophy for action, no individual behavior, even, can guarantee acceptance—much less protection. We obviously need to be wary of idealistic thinking here. It will never prevent raiders from attacking members of relief organizations or political-military leaders from targeting humanitarian organizations in order to deter, pressure, or manipulate them.

Nevertheless, it is important to think principles out—for starters because it is essential in and of itself, especially in an increasingly perplexing time such as the present. Provided, naturally, that principles should be treated not as abstractions but as the materials for critical thinking.

Also because adherence to certain principles of action—not by expressing them as generalities but by routinely factoring them into decisions and actions on the ground—may perhaps allow us to better orient ourselves and establish more clearly defined relationships with local and international actors.

So I'm going to quickly outline the principles we think are important. I'll be fairly brief because I believe it is difficult, perhaps even fruitless, to speak of principles in the abstract. They have to be tied to experiences—something that isn't easy to do in the few minutes I have remaining.

So I'll just describe a few concrete applications of principles relating to the issue of security we are discussing here today.

Impartiality

I'll begin with neutrality, which will allow me—and this won't surprise you—to offer a point of view different from that of the ICRC. And I'm raising the issue specifically in order to rule it out as a principle for action.

MSF has had many discussions on this topic over a number of years, without coming to any definitive conclusion. Still, a lot us do agree it does not involve any kind of absolute dictate or principle. Of course we fully believe that, in the majority of conflicts, we have no business taking sides with this or that belligerent party. This doesn't mean we can remain neutral or silent when confronted with genocide or an oppressive regime. So for us neutrality is something that varies according to the situation, not a guiding principle. Or, if it is a principle, it is a passive one, not a principle of action …

In contrast, we see impartiality as an essential principle in humanitarian action. It posits that a wounded soldier, a combatant not involved in combat, if only temporarily—in short, a man, woman, or child in need must be assisted without discrimination. Being impartial, then, means assisting any person in need according to their need, without regard to race, religion, nationality, or political affiliation.

On a concrete level this means assessing needs in a fully independent manner and monitoring how aid is distributed in order to ensure it isn't diverted from its targets and that it truly reaches those for whom it is intended. Naturally, needs assessment is not the be-all and end-all; it needs to be paired with a more comprehensive analysis of the causes of the target population's deteriorating situation, particularly to determine whether it is the result of any strategy on the part of political authorities, as may be the case, for example, when famine has been induced or is being sustained.

Whatever the cause, an independent assessment of needs and strict monitoring of aid distribution are vital for delivering assistance impartially. As I have described it, this obligation of fairness is very different from the notion of even-handedness between parties that can be dictated by a false conception of neutrality.

Human Concern

Humanitarian aid aims to preserve life in dignity and respect; it attempts to deliver aid in a time of crisis and to give back to people their capacity for choice.

In other words, in contrast to development aid, humanitarian aid does not seek to devise any sort of project for society or spark some bold transformation of a way of life. Nor does it claim to offer comprehensive solutions to conflicts.

By putting it in these terms I mean to emphasize that humanitarian action is rooted in a humanist ethic. It intervenes on a human scale. But, again, humanist principles are nothing but abstractions emptied of meaning if they do not translate into behavior, ways of being and doing.

From this perspective, admittedly, we face a lot of issues because the aid system has evolved significantly. It now attracts substantial resources. This infusion of wealth and goods, apparently free of charge in a context of extreme scarcity, amounts to a kind of symbolic violence that in itself is a source of tension. This is not without consequences for humanitarian organizations, especially in full-blown crisis situations.

Also because certain types of interventions, certain mechanistic practices focused on technical efficiency alone, can at times breed attitudes of arrogance and contempt.

Respect for human dignity is at times not really compatible with mass-oriented operations. The "assisted populations" and "vulnerable groups" frequently referenced in the jargon of relief workers are not, it must be remembered, clusters of physiological organisms. Humanitarian action has nothing to do with some sort of veterinary compassion. The concern for others that guides us applies to human beings, not to digestive apparatuses.

In many situations we may need to be able to abandon certain technocratic ways of operating, certain stereotypical, large-scale types of operations, certain methods of population "management." At times we may have to be able to resist pressure from financial donors and—always—our own organizational cultures.

It is time to reopen the dialogue, to recover a responsiveness and sense of closeness in our relations with the individuals we are helping, those we work and interact with.

In this regard—and returning to the question of security—it might be helpful to recall that the quality of our relationships with local staff clearly is an important factor in how well we understand their societies and, it goes without saying, the quality of information and assistance they can provide us in case of difficulty.

Independence

For us, independence is a core principle, which many of the others depend upon. It has come up throughout this brief outline I've been giving: independent needs assessment, independence with regard to financial donors and our own institutional interests, free and open dialogue with individuals, and so on.

Independence is not a principle to be proclaimed: it is not an institutional position to take with respect to financial donors or a moral stance to assume in dealing with political-military warlords or military-economic entrepreneurs. Independence is a way of relating to authority, one that is by definition antagonistic.

By putting it this way I do not mean it is aggressive; I'm speaking of the tension inherent in all relations between citizens, or associations of citizens, and authority. This tension is all the more acute in full-blown crisis situations. In such cases it is no longer mediated by delegation or consent. It is often aggravated and gets expressed through force or constraint.

In these highly politically charged crisis situations involving rights abuses, "victimist" strategies, and the exploitation of aid, humanitarian organizations must continually negotiate, resist, maneuver, refuse, condemn, and so on.

Tensions run high in conflict situations, and how we deal with authority is extremely critical for organizations attempting to deliver aid impartially. In certain situations one has to be able to say no and go public with bad news.

Dealing with political authority is problematic in Western countries as well. States, and by extension financial donors, act (legitimately from their point of view) according to their national interests, though they may not be impervious to the calls for solidarity emerging within their own societies.

Humanitarian organizations, whose intentions are profoundly different, are obviously under no obligation to always respond to appeals from states.

Too often, unfortunately, humanitarian actors go along with the policies of donor nations, at the risk of seeming to be associated with governments. The fact that their organizational cultures very often adapt easily to the role of subcontractor makes this easier.

Here again the politics of supply, which creates a framework wherein programs are judged by how much funding they can attract, does not always support the kinds of decisions that might follow from an independent assessment of the situation and of opportunities for intervention.

But independence is neither a rhetorical posture nor a moralistic formula to be invoked against authority. It requires critical reflection, and this has to start with ourselves.

At minimum—and MSF is not exempt from this criticism—humanitarian organizations are frequently not vigilant enough. They are lacking in critical spirit, in the capacity for self-questioning. Too often they reflexively adhere to fashionable clichés, all the more willingly because their institutional interests frequently coincide with the prevailing winds. Self righteous rhetoric, good intentions, and moralistic posing can become a kind of ambient background noise, dulling our vigilance and deadening our awareness of our responsibilities.

As MSF found in Ethiopia and in Rwanda's refugee camps, and as other humanitarian organizations have experienced on other occasions, it can be very costly—in terms of image, funding, institutional relationships, and relations with authorities—to depart from lukewarm consensus and adopt a critical stance. But, then, independence has its price ...

Index

A

Abkhazia, 90
Activist refugees, 95 (n1)
Addis Ababa, 6, 7, 10, 13, 154
  accords of, 56
Afghanistan, 77, 118, 142
  conflicts in, 50, 69, 144, 150, 151
  François Jean in, vi
  humanitarian aid for, 130, 142, 146
  nonintervention in, 89
  refugee camps in, 137
  refugees from, 96, 99
Africa
  exports from, 128, 144
  humanitarian aid for, 130
  peacemaking operations in, 91
  refugee policy for, 105
African Great Lakes region
  crisis in, 154-155
  safety in, 142
Africans, Islamized, 58
agricultural factory, myth of, 6
AICF, 109, 110
Aidid, Mohammed Farrah, 53
aid worker safety, 61, 142
Albania, 28
Algeria, humanitarian aid refusal by, 141, 142
American Mineral Fields, 128-129
Andersson, Nils, conversation with, 114-124
Angola
  humanitarian aid to, 139, 142, 144
  MSF role in, 59-60
  peacemaking operations in, 91
  UN operations in, 83
animism, 56
Arab dissuasion Force, 90
Argun, conflict in, 68, 69
Armagnac, 35(n15)
Armed Forces of Rwanda (ex-FAR), 143
Arusha group, 155
asylum, rights to, 102-104
asylum politics, for refugees, 95
Austria, refugee asylum in, 102

B

Baggara, 56
Bank of Korea, 28
Barre, Siad, 50, 53, 69
Bassaev, Shamil, 72, 74
Beijing, 37
  NGO conference at, 153
Beirut, 69
Bellefroid, Vincent de, 63
Bengal, 42
  refugees from, 96
Berlin Wall, 95
  fall of, 84, 93, 107, 108
Bettati, Mario, conversation with, 107-113
Biafran conflict, 149, 150

Blue Helmets, 61, 83, 109, 110, 118, 119, 120
  in Cambodia, 122
  Nobel Prize for, 82
  in Somalia, 91-92
boat people
  from Albania, 97
  from Vietnam, 96, 150
Bonino, Emma, 162
Bosnia
  conflict in, 56, 117, 144, 150
  ethnic cleansing in, 126
  humanitarian aid to, 62, 135(n14), 139, 140, 146
  intervention in, 102, 111, 119
  military interventions in, 91, 92, 118
  MSF role in, 59-60
  political dilemmas in, 112
  refugees from, 93, 100, 102, 103, 104
  Security Council resolution on, 85
  UN operations in, 83, 89
Botlikh, Wahhabis in, 72-73
Boutros-Ghali, Boutros, 85, 88, 153(n39)
Brauman, Rony, iv, vi, 116
Bread Procurement Commission, 8
brotherhood of victims, 162
Bukharin, N. I., 6-7
Burma, 118
  minority repression in, 86, 101
  refugees from, 93, 94
Burundi, 155(n40)
  murders in, 61
  refugees from, 109
  war in, 128

C

Calot, G., 5
Cambodia
  Blue Helmets in, 122
  peacemaking operations in, 91, 109
  refugees repatriation in, 99
  transition periods in, 144
  UN operations in, 83, 89
Cartagena Declaration of 1984, 96, 105
Carter, Jimmy, 154
Carter Center, 155
Caucasus
  destabilization of, 79
  intervention in, 87, 90
Central America, peacemaking operations in, 91
Chagan, famine refugees in, 45
Charachidze, Georges, 75
Chatoi, MSF in, 65, 67, 69
Chechen Republic of Ichkeria, 73
Chechnya
  François Jean in, vi, 63-64
  human rights debacle in, 71
  kidnappings in, 61
  medical relief problems in, 66-70, 143
  MSF aid to, 63-65

  murders in, 61
  NGOS in, 67, 68
  Russian peace accord with, 65
  Russian "reconquest" of, 74
  Russian revenge in, 73-80
  "security zone" in, 77
  solutions for, 79-80
  war in, vi, 73-80
China, 34
  collectivization in, 7
  Cultural Revolution of, 31
  famine in, v, 3, 4, 5, 11-12, 25, 27, 37, 41
  famine refugees in, 45, 47, 48
  Great Leap Forward of, 11-12, 26, 27, 31, 42
  trade with North Korea, 35-36, 37, 42
Ch'llima Movement, 31
Chongsanri method, 31
"clan war", 77
cognac, 35(n15)
Cold War, vii, 50, 59, 61, 83, 84, 86, 91, 93, 95, 96, 100, 127, 131
  aftermath of, 125-126, 130, 138, 139, 150-152, 159
  humanitarian aid in, 150
  United Nations and, 119
Communism, collapse of, 94
Communist Party, famine and, 8
Community of Sant'Edigio, 155
concealed famine, 41-43
concentration camps, Nazi, 5
conflict, 49-80
  humanitarian aid role in dynamics of, 140-144
  privatization roles in, 87
  security and, 50-52
  in Somalia, 53-55
  in Sudan, 56-58
  UN intervention in, 87
Congo, 86
Conquest, R., 5
containment strategies, 100-102
corn, trade in, 35
Council of Europe, 80
criminalized guerilla fighter, 126
Croatia
  humanitarian aid to, 135(n14)
  refugees from, 93, 100, 102, 103, 104
  UN troops in, 85
Cultural Revolution, of China, 31

D

DAC. *See* Development Assistance Committee (DAC)
Dagestan
  MSF work in, 66
  Wahhabis in, 72-73
Darfur, conflict in, 58
Da'wa Islamiya, 148
decolonization, after WWII, 129
de facto refugees, 104
de-*kulakization*, 5

Democratic Republic, 13
Department of Humanitarian Affairs (UN), 135(n13)
Deresa, Berhane, 22(n13)
de-Stalinization, famine and, 3
Development Assistance Committee (DAC), 131
Disaster Relief Teams, 135(n14)
Doctors Without Borders. *See* Médecins Sans Frontières (MSF)
Doe, Samuel, 50
drought
  in Ethiopia, 13, 20, 57
  in Kenya, 20
  in North Korea, 39
Dublin convention, 103

E
East Pakistan, 90
ECHO. *See* European Commission's Humanitarian Aid Office (ECHO)
"economic migrants", refugees as, vii
ECRE. *See* European Council on Refugees and Exiles (ECRE)
ECUs, 18
EEC/EU. *See* European Economic Community (EEC)
Egypt, 54, 57
El Salvador
  peacemaking operations in, 91, 109
  refugee repatriation in, 99
  UN operations in, 83
emergency aid, 131
Eritrea
  conflict in, 12-13, 147
  famine in, 10, 12
  NGOs in, 149, 150
Ethiopia
  aid to, 17-18, 20, 144, 167
  conflict in, 159
  drought in, 13, 20, 57
  famine in, iv, v, 2, 3, 4, 5, 10-11, 25, 57
  François Jean in, vi
  MSF expulsion from, 12, 19
  NGOs in, 149
  political famine in, 12-23
  quest of funds by, 15-17
  refugees in, 100
Ethiopian National Central Planning Committee, 10(n5)
ethnic cleansing, 87, 92, 100, 105
Europe, refugees in, 93-106
European Commission's Humanitarian Aid Office (ECHO), 131, 133, 135, 154, 157
  emergency aid of, 158
European Community Task Force (ECTF), 135(n14)
European Council on Refugees and Exiles (ECRE), 105(n6)
European Economic Community (EEC), 17, 18, 90
European Union, 70

F
Face aux Crises (Jean), 107
famine, 1-10
  in China, 3, 11-12, 26, 27, 37, 41
  Chinese refugees from, 45
  concealed, 41-43
  deaths from, 2, 4-5, 25-26
  in Eritrea, 10, 12
  in Ethiopia, iv, v, 2, 3, 4, 5, 10-11, 25, 57
  food self-reliance leading to, 33-36
  ideology and, 2-12
  in Kazakhstan, 5, 27
  in Northern Caucasus, 2
  in North Korea, 26, 27, 41-43, 46
  politically-inspired, 3-5
  in Russia, 3, 37, 41
  in Somalia, 25, 26
  in Sudan, 25, 26
  in Tigre, 10, 12
  in Ukraine, v, 2, 3, 5, 26, 27
  in USSR, 7, 27
ex-FAR. *See* Armed Forces of Rwanda (ex-FAR)
Fifth Workers' Party Conference (1970), 44
filtration camps, 76
flooding, in North Korea, 39, 40
Fondation, vi, 63
FPLE. *See* Popular Front for the Liberation of Eritrea (FPLE)
France
  asylum seekers in, 98, 104
  Ethiopian aid and, 17
  humanitarian aid and politics in, 154
  humanitarian aid of, 135, 137
  freedom fighters, 97, 137

G
Gantemirov, Besian, 78
Garang, John, 56
GDP, of North Korea, 27, 34
Geneva Conventions, 50, 51, 69, 70, 109, 110, 116-117, 118,
  genocide, massacre as, 111
Georgia, 118
  Blue Helmets in, 82
Germany
  emergency aid of, 131(n7)
  refugee asylum in, 102
  reunification of, 37, 38
Giorgis, Dawit Wolde, 22
GPU, 8, 9
grain
  Chinese production of, 11
  Ethiopian production of, 14
  North Korean production of, 28
  supply to Ethiopia, 16(n3)
  Ukraine production of, 8-9
Great Britain
  emergency aid of, 131 (n7)
  Ethiopian aid and, 17
Greater Liberia, 128
Great Famine, in China, 3, 5
Great Lakes region (Africa), crisis in, 154-155

Great Leader, of North Korea, 29, 31, 32, 44
Great Leap Forward (China), 11-12, 26, 27, 31, 42
  mortality from, 5
  "great leap forward" (Ethiopia), 21
Gromov, Boris, 75
Grozny
  MSF aid to, 63-64
  refugees from, 68
  war in, vi, 64
Gudermes, conflict in, 68, 69, 72
guerilla activities, 137
  effects on humanitarian aid, 59, 126
  in Eritrea and Tigre, 23
Gulf War, 88

H
Haiti, 90, 101, 154
Halifax, G7 summit in, 70
Hama, 69
Hamgyong, famine refugees in, 45
Hammarskjöld, Dag, 83
Hanoi, 90
Hargeisa, 69
Helsinki Agreements, 84
Herriot, Edouard, 9, 26
Holland, emergency aid of, 131(n7)
The Holocaust, 9
Honduras, contras in, 137
hospitals, in Chechnya, 64
Hoxha, Enver, 28
human rights movement, 84-85
human rights organizations, role in humanitarian aid, 72
human rights "revolution", 115
humanitarian action
  compromised, 114-124
  politics and, 107-113
humanitarian aid
  emergency aid and, 133
  human concern of, 165-166
  impartiality of, 164-165
  independence role in, 166-167
  internalization of, 136-140
  to North Korea, 39-41
  political support for, 130-132
  principles of action of, 157-167
  redeployment of, 158-163
  role in conflict dynamics, 140-144, 146
  security and, 157-167
humanitarianism, success of, 131-132
humanitarian law, Chechnyan conflicts and, 69
humanitarian sanctuaries, 97
  refugee camps as, 137, 140, 142
Hungary, refugee asylum in, 102

I
IARA. *See* Islamic Relief Agency (IARA)
Ichkeria, Chechen Republic of, 73
ICRC. *See* International Committee of the Red Cross (ICRC)
IGAD. *See* Intergovernmental Authority and Development (IGAD)
India, Pakistani intervention by, 90

169

Ingushetia, MSF work in, 66
insecurity zones, 145
Intergovernmental Authority and
  Development (IGAD), 154
international aid, 81-167
  to North Korea, 36, 39-41
  security for, 61
International Alert, 155
International Committee of the Red
  Cross (ICRC), 64, 103, 109, 118, 121,
  137, 141, 143, 149, 157, 164
"international community", MSF role
  in, vii
International Crisis Group, 155
International Labor Office, 16
International Monetary Fund (IMF), 148
intervention, right of, 107(n1)
intervention strategies, 100-102
Iran-Iraq conflict, 4
Iraq, viii
  humanitarian aid for, 135(n14),
    139, 140
  intervention in, 85, 88-89, 91, 102,
    118, 130
  MSF role in, 59-60
  refugees from, 101
  Resolution 688 on, 85, 99, 114-115, 152
  transition periods in, 144
Islam
  in Chechnya, 72
  fundamentalist groups of. See Wahhabis
  in Sudan, 147-148
Islamic Relief Agency (IARA), 148
Islamists NGOs, 148
Italy, boat people in, 97

J
Japan, 34
  aid from, 36
  humanitarian aid of, 155(n41)
Jean, François
  conversations with, 107-113, 114-124
  humanitarianism of, v
  role in MSF, iv
Juche faming method, 31

K
Kabila, Laurent-Desiré, 129
Kabul, refugees from, 99
Kagame, Paul, 143
Kalashnikovs, security and, 50
Kazakhstan, famine in, 5, 27
Kenya
  aid to, 20
  refugees in, 100
KGB, 8
Khartoum, refugees in, 57, 58
Khasavyurt Accords of 1996, 71, 73
Khattah, Emir, 72
Khmer Rouge, 90, 99, 137
  social regeneration and, 5
Khrushchev, Nikita, 7
kidnappings, 61, 142
Kiev, 6
Kim Dae Jung, 39
Kim Il Sung, 29, 30, 31, 32, 34, 35,
  37, 44, 47

Kim Jong-il, 31(n11)
Kim Young Sam, 37
Kinshasa, 129
Kiriyenko, Sergei, 73
Kivu, 139, 143
kolkhozes, 6
Kordofan, refugees in, 57
Korea, 88
Korean Buddhist Sharing Movement,
  48(n24)
Korean War, 32, 44
Kremlin. See Russia/Soviet Union
kulak, 6
Kurdistan, 130
  transitional periods in, 144
Kurds, 88-89, 101, 114, 116
  humanitarian aid for, 140
  as refugees, 135(n14)
Kurtchaloi, MSF work in, 67
Kuwait, aggression wars on, 86, 88
Kvashnin, Anatoly, 75

L
Lapérou, Cécile, iv
Latin America, refugee policy for, 105
Lebanon, 86, 90, 143
  conflict in, 147
  MSF in, v
Lebed Alexander, 73, 79
Le Devoir d'Ingèrence (Bettati), 107
Le Page, Marie, iv
Liberation Army/SPLA, 56, 58, 134(n12)
Liberation Tigers of Tamil Eelam
  (LTTE), 148
Liberia
  aid to, 144, 146
  conflict in, 87
  foreign trade by, 128
  Nigerian intervention of, 90
  refugees from, 100
  security in, 50-52, 142
Liberté Sans Frontières, vi
Life, Death, and Aid (Jean), 89
Lome Convention III, 17, 18
  looting, war financed by, 87
LTTE. See Liberiation Tigers of Tamil
  Eelam (LTTE)
Lyssenko, Trofim, 31

M
Mace, J., 5
al-Mahdi, Sadek, 56
Makhno, 8
Maoism, 113
Mao Tse-tung, 26, 32
Marketi, MSF work in, 67
Marx, Karl, 6
Maskhadov, Aslan, 72, 73, 74, 78, 80
mass extermination, famine and, 4
Massoud, Ahmad, 150(n35)
Médecins Sans Frontières (MSF), 116,
  121, 163,
  charter of, ii, 51
  in Chechnya, 63-64
  Ethiopian expulsion of, 12, 19
  François Jean in, vi-viii, 63
  impartiality and, 164

roles of
  in Angola, 59-60
  in Bosnia, 59-60
  in Iraq, 59-60
  in Somalia, vii, 51, 54, 59-60
  medical relief, in Chechen war zones,
    66-70
Mengistu, Haile Mariam, 6, 7, 14, 15,
  16, 18, 21
military-humanitarian operations, 160
military interventions, 91-92
Mitterand, François, 26
mixed intervention force, 90
Mogadishu, conflict in, 53-54, 110,
  111, 112
Mohammed, Ali Mahdi, 53
Mongolia, food shortages in, 27
Mozambique
  aid to, 144
  conflicts in, 50, 155
  peacemaking operations in, 91
Mugunga camp, attack on, 142
mujik, 6
murders, 61, 142
mushrooms, North Korean sales of, 35
Muslims
  in Bosnia, 100
  as refugees, 93
Mussolini, Benito, 58

N
Najibullah regime, fall of, 99
Namibia, refugee repatriation in, 99
Naqshbandiya brotherhood, in
  Chechnya, 72
National Coordinating Committee for
  Villagization, 19
National Islamic Front, 57
National Patriotic Front of Liberia
  (NPFL), 128
National Union for Total
  Independence of Angola (UNITA),
  128, 146(n30), 150
Naurskaya, 74
Nazi concentration camps of, 5
Naziism, 94
Nazran, 65
  MSF work in, 66
neutrality, humanitarian aid and, 51
New Economic Policy (NEP), 8, 10, 18
Niger, famine in, v
Nigeria, intervention by, 90
Nobel Peace Prize, 82
nongovernmental organizations
  (NGOs), vii, 40
  activity in conflict zones, 61, 108-109,
    110, 113, 121, 123-124
  in Chechnya, 67
  in Ethiopia, 23
  humanitarian aid of, 133, 134, 136,
    162-163
  international conferences of, 153
  Islamist, 148
  quasi-official roles of, vii, 40, 155
  redeployment of aid by, 158-163
  role in policy-making, 154
  Russian Federation and, 141

in Southern Hemisphere countries, 147
non-state actors, increasing power of,
132-136
Northern Caucasus
famine in, 2
MSF work in, 66-70
North Korea
agriculture in, 30
bankrupt economy of, 30-33, 38
chronic scarcity in, 28-30
famine in, v, 26, 27, 38, 41-43, 46
famine regime in, 24-48
food trade of, 35
hierarchical society of, 44
international aid to, 36, 39-41, 43
scarcity and rationing in, 43-45
South Korea and, 37
North Ossetia, MSF work in, 66
North Wallo, conflict in, 13
NPFL. See National Patriotic Front of
Liberia (NPFL)
nuclear blackmail, by Pyongyang, 36
nuclear proliferation treaty,
Pyongyang and, 24
Nuremburg war crimes tribunal, 117

O
OAS. See Organization of American
States (OAS)
OAU. See Organization of African
Unity (OAU)
ODA. See Official Development
Assistance (ODA)
OECD. See Organization for Economic
Cooperation and Development
(OECD)
Official Development Assistance
(ODA), 131, 133, 135(n14)
oil, North Korean imports of, 33
Operation Lifeline Sudan (OLS),
139, 160
Operation Provide Comfort, 140
Organization for Economic
Cooperation and Development
(OECD), 131, 133
Organization for Security and
Cooperation in Europe (OSCE),
80, 141
Organization of African Unity (OAU),
89-90, 96, 155
1969 convention of, 96, 105
Organization of American States
(OAS), 90
OSCE. See Organization for Security
and Cooperation in Europe (OSCE)
Oslo process, 154
Ossetia, 90
Ould-Abdallah, Ahmedou, 155(n40)
Ourlanis, B., 4

P
pacification strategy, Chechnya, 79
Pakistan, 90
refugee camps in, 137
refugees in, 99
Palestine, vi
Panmunjom, truce accord of, 40

parallel diplomacy, 149-156
Paris accords of 1991, 99
peacekeeping by Security Council,
82-90
peacemaking, 91, 130
peasants
in Ethiopia, 14-15, 19
extermination by hunger, 7-9
social consciousness and, 5
Perez de Cuellar, Javier, 85
Peru, conflict in, 144
Petiville, Stéphen de, 58
Phelan, Kevin P. Q., v-viii
Poles, as refugees, 93
politics, humanitarian action and,
107-113, 130-132
Popular Front for the Liberation of
Eritrea (FPLE), 150
population displacements, 22
in Ethiopia, 19
Populations in Danger (Jean), vi
Prigorodny, MSF work in, 66
privatization
of public services, 144-149
role in wars, 87
protection rackets, 145
Provide Comfort, Restore Hope
operation, 160
Public Distribution System (PDS), of
international aid, 43, 45
public services, privatization of, 144-149
Pulikovsky, Konstantin, 75
Putin, Vladimir, 74
Pyongyang, 36, 37, 38, 40, 41, 46
food aid to, 42

Q
Qadiriya Sufi brotherhood, in
Chechnya, 72

R
racketeering, war financed by 87
"radiant future", of Ethiopia, 13
Reagan, Ronald, economic policy
of, 39
Red Cross. See International
Committee of the Red Cross (ICRC)
redeployment, of humanitarian aid,
158-163
refugee camps, as humanitarian sanctuaries, 137, 140, 160
refugees
in Cold War, vii
containment strategies for, 100-102
OAU definition of, 96(n2)
policy for, 104-106
solutions for, 98-100
three ages of, 94-98
world population of, 93
rice
North Korea rationing of, 45
trade in, 35
"Rice-Socialism", 29
right of intervention, 107(n1)
Rio de Janeiro, NGO conference
at, 153
Rio Environmental Summit, 57

Rohingyas, as refugees, 93
Romanians, as refugees, 93
Rural Theses, of Kim Il Sung, 31
Russia/Soviet Union, 16, 32, 33, 34
agriculture failure in, 7
breakup of, 39, 141
colonialism of, 71
conflict with Chechnya, 66-70
conflict with Grozny, 63-65
famine deaths in, 5
famine in, 3, 5, 7, 27, 37, 41
humanitarian groups in, 141, 142, 143
peacekeeping by, 90
peasant agriculture in, 10
refugees from, 93
Rwanda
Blue Helmets in, 82
humanitarian aid for, 140
intervention in, 87
murders in, 61, 70, 150
NGOs in, 149
refugee camps in, 138, 142-143, 167

S
Sahel, famine in, 3
Samashki, 65
San Francisco Charter, 82
Sarajevo, 69, 110
Scandanavia, humanitarian aid of,
155(n41)
Schengen convention, 103
seafood, North Korean sales of, 35
security, for international groups,
50, 61
Security Council
peacekeeping by, 82-83, 86-90
resolutions of, 112, 114, 117, 118,
139, 152
Security Council Resolution 688, 85,
99, 114, 153
Security Council Resolution 770, 85
Security Council Resolution 794,
85, 114
Sen, Amartya, 43
Seoul, 37, 38, 40
Serbs
in Bosnia, 100
as refugees, 93, 104
Sernovodsk, 65
Shali, conflict in, 68, 69
Shamanov, Vladmir, 75
Shelkovskaya, 74
Shiites, 88, 101
Sierra Leone, 128, 144
"social prophylaxis", 4
social regeneration, 5
social transformation, famine and, v
Somalia
Blue Helmets in, 85-86, 92
crisis in, 86
famine in, 25, 26
François Jean in, vi
GIs in, 86
humanitarian aid to, vii, viii, 54-55,
62, 82, 85, 91, 109, 110, 121, 122,
138, 142, 144, 146, 161
intervention in, 85, 90, 91, 92, 110, 118

MSF role in, 59-60
refugees from, 93, 94
Security Council resolution 794 on, 85, 114
security in, 50-52
UN operations in, 83, 89, 90
South Africa, Blue Helmets in, 82
Southeast Asia, peacemaking operations in, 91
Southern Hemisphere
NGOs in, 148
refugees from, 95, 96, 98, 102
threat of, 141
South Korea, 34, 37, 44
aid from, 36
Soviet Union. *See* Russia/Soviet Union
sovkohzes, 6
"spiritual pollution", 40
SPLA. *See* Sudanese People's Liberation Army (SPLA)
Sputnik province (China), 12
Sri Lanka
humanitarian aid for, 130, 147
Indian intervention in, 90, 101
NGOs in, 148
Stalin, Josef, 5, 6, 15, 72
Stalinism, 113
starvation, in North Korea, 47-48
steel, Chinese production of, 11
Stroumlin, S., 6
subsistence agriculture in Ethiopia, 10
Sudan, 118, 142
conflict in, 56-58, 147, 151, 154
famine in, 25, 26
François Jean in, vi
humanitarian aid to, 121, 134(n12), 144
Islamist NGOs in, 148
nonintervention in, 89
refugees from, 93
Sudanese People's Liberation Army (SPLA), 56, 58, 134(n12)
sunshine policy, of South Korea, 39
Sweden, Ethiopian aid and, 17
Swedish Agency for Development, 17
Syria, intervention in Lebanon by, 90

T
Taif Agreements, 90
Tajikstan
Blue Helmets in, 82
François Jean in, vi
intervention in, 87, 90
kidnappings in, 61
refugees from, 93
The Tale of Igor's Armament, 2
Tamils, humanitarian aid for, 90
Tanzania, refugee camps in, 138
Tanzanian intervention, in Uganda, 85
target refugees, 95(nl)
Taylor, Charles, 128
Three Revolution Teams, 31
Tiananmen Square, 39
Tigre
conflict in, 12-13
famine in, 10, 12
Tilly Charles, 129
Tokyo, 37

Tolotti, Sandrine, 113
tractor(s)
cult of, 6
North Korean manufacture of, 32-33
trafficking, war financed by, 87
Transalls, 111
transition periods, 144
transnational mafia, 126
Tsumada, Wahhabis in, 72-73
al-Turabi, Hassan, 57
Turkey, Kurdish refugees and, 101

U
Uganda
civil war in, 126
Tanzanian intervention in, 85
Ukraine
de-Stalinization in, 3
extermination by hunger in, 7-9
famine deaths in, 26
famine in, v, 2, 3, 5, 7-9, 26, 27
UN High Commissioner of Refugees (UNHCR), 94, 95-96, 97, 102, 105, 110, 121
UNICEF, 121, 139(n22)
UNITA. *See* National Union for Total Independence of Angola (UNITA)
United Nations, vii, 26, 39, 40, 58, 60, 112
activity in conflict zones, 61-62
Blue Helmets of. *see* Blue Helmets
charter of, 84, 89, 116
Department of Humanitarian Affairs, 154
food aid from, 36
High Commissioner of Human Rights, 154
humanitarian aid of, 133, 139, 152, 158-160
international aid and, 82
intervention by, 119
new role for, 82-84
nonintervention by, 89
refugees and, 99
regional intervention by, 89-90
Security Council of. *See* Security Council
sovereignty and intervention by, 84-86
United States
African trade of, 128
GIs sent to Somalia by, 86
humanitarian aid of, 131(n7), 134, 135, 155
refugee resettlement in, 95
State Department, 154
Universal Declaration of Human Rights, 112, 113
UNOSOM Blue Helmets, 118
US Coast Guard, boat people and, 97
USSR. *See* Russia/Soviet Union

V
victimhood strategies, 150-152
Vietnam, 32
boat people from, 96, 150
Cambodian invasion by, 85, 90
food shortages in, 27
refugees from, 96
Vietnam Syndrom, 97
Vietnam War, 96
villagization, 19
violence-victim refugees, 95(n1)

W
Wahhabis, in Chechnya, 72
War Communism, 7, 8
Washington, D.C., 37, 40
Westphalia treaty, 84
whales, publicity on death of, 57
wheat flour, trade in, 35
Workers' Party, 13
World Bank, 11, 17, 22, 95
World Food Program (WFP), 121, 133(n9)
World War I, 2
World War II, 2, 26, 84, 102, 106, 129
deaths from, 4

Y
Yalta, 84
Yanggang, famine refugees in, 45
Yeltsin, Boris, 73, 78
Yemen, refugees in, 100
Yugoslavia, 42, 59, 90
detainees in, 42, 59, 90, 103
humanitarian aid for, 140
intervention in, 87
ex-Yugoslavia
intervention in, 102, 104, 118, 130
refugees from, 94, 100, 104
refugees in, 100

Z
Zaire
foreign trade by, 128
humanitarian aid for, 130, 135
intervention in, 87
refugee camps in, 138
ex-Zaire, 143, 144
Zolberg, Aristide R., refugee classification of, 95(n1)